RECKLESS
HOPE

RECKLESS
HOPE

*Understanding and Reaching
Baby Busters*

**Todd Hahn
and
David Verhaagen**

Foreword by Leighton Ford

Baker Books

A Division of Baker Book House Co
Grand Rapids, Michigan 49516

Rev. Tom Tate 2014

Published by Baker Books
a division of Baker Book House Company
P.O. Box 6287, Grand Rapids, MI 49516-6287

Printed in the United States of America

Library of Congress Cataloging-in-Publication Data

Hahn, Todd, 1968–
    Reckless hope : understanding and reaching baby busters /
Todd Hahn & David Verhaagen.
       p. cm.
    Includes bibliographical references.
    ISBN 0-8010-9018-0 (paper)
    1. Church work with young adults. 2. Generation X—Psychol-
ogy. 3. Generation X—Religious life. 4. Evangelistic work. 5. Intergenerational relations. I. Verhaagen, David. II. Title.
    BV4446.H35 1996
    259'.23—dc20   96-33887

Contents

Foreword

They say that nostalgia is one sure sign of getting older. Well, if so, reading *Reckless Hope* has made me nostalgic, but at the same time it has made me feel young!

Authors Todd Hahn and David Verhaagen have a passionate longing to engage their generation with the hope of Christ. In that they remind me of the young followers of Christ I grew up with in the late 40s and early 50s.

Like Todd and David we, too, wanted to spread the gospel to our contemporaries and became part of the burgeoning youth evangelistic movements of that day.

At mid-century we were part of a postwar world waiting to be reborn. Now at end-century the Baby Busters are part of what is often called a postmodern world that is emerging.

But there is a significant difference. In the aftermath of World War II there was tremendous optimism about the future. We knew things were going to be better for us than they were for our parents. But the Baby Busters have no such confidence. Often distrusting of science, disillusioned by religion, let down by their own parents, manipulated by the media, they have been described as "hopeless, have not, and pain filled."

So today's youth are more than a cohort of young people who wear their baseball caps backward. They may well be the vanguard of a vast cultural, philosophical shift. They question not only whether truth is absolute or relative but whether it exists at all.

Yet it is truly a sign of the "reckless hope" this book espouses that it has been written by two young men who know the heart of this generation.

I have known Todd Hahn for years—as a promising college student introduced to me by my son, as a gifted young writer and pastor, as the editor of a newsletter for young leaders published by our ministry—and he is about the last person I can imagine wearing his cap backward! But he and his psychologist buddy, David, are in touch with the hearts and not just the fads of their peers.

Two words describe this book for me: "timely" and "timeless." "Timely" because it paints such a vivid portrait of this generation, and "timeless" because it addresses the needs and hungers of this generation with the eternal hope of Christ.

Reckless Hope is a fine sociological analysis of the so-called Buster generation. But it does something far more daring—it asserts unapologetically that theology and not just methodology and marketing is crucial if pre-Christian Busters are to be intersected with new hope.

Building a strong biblical foundation, the authors show how key theological concepts speak powerfully to this generation—concepts like creation (for a generation concerned about the environment), covenant (for a generation that has grown up on broken promises), and community (for a generation hungering for true family).

Two other words also come to mind. This book is *lively*—interesting and gripping, and it is *passionate*—with its call for heroic discipleship.

Reckless Hope should be read by those of any age and all generations who want to introduce the God of hope to those who will inherit the coming millennium.

Leighton Ford

Preface

Todd: In what I dearly hope was not a Freudian-prophetic slip of the tongue, my wife, Jane, recently referred to this book as "Hopeless Wreck." The irony is that, in many minds, this would be a nearly perfect description of our generation.

We wrote this book because of our fundamental conviction that our generation is not now and does not have to become a hopeless wreck. In spite of its painful past and uncertain future, we believe that Generation X holds almost unlimited hope for the future of the church and the world.

In his role as a psychologist, Dave sees the reality of emotional and mental pain in the lives of many Baby Busters. In my role as a pastor, I see the painful effects of our generation's loss of spiritual connectedness in terms of relationships and life integration. Even in the face of what we see on a daily basis, we affirm together that there is hope, that this hope is found only in Christ, and that our generation is uniquely positioned to be transmitters of hope to an increasingly hopeless world.

I am grateful to Leighton Ford, a mentor and encourager. Without his help, this book would not have been completed and published.

Kevin Ford, Bill Haley, and Dieter Zander have been pacesetters and thought provokers for me in thinking through how to reach Busters with the gospel. My colleagues at Forest Hill practice passionate and effective ministry and are also wonderful friends. Leadership Community and coreX are a living laboratory for the values of community, people, culture, and change. Kurt and Kathi Graves, Sean and Christine Meade, and Bill and Roxanne Morgan are great friends and partners in ministry. Paul Engle and Mary Suggs of Baker have been truly helpful servants, as has my dedicated and omnicompetent assistant, Pamela Fox. My parents, Bill and Elaine Hahn, have always encouraged and loved me. Robbi Fischer, Dave Grigg, Steve Haimbaugh, Eric Hauser, Tom Hawkes, Matt Kern, Pat Sawyer, Roger Severino, Hank Tarlton, and Richard Wilson have all been friends and encouragers in varied ways and for varied numbers of years! They all share a part in this book.

Dave Verhaagen is a close and valued friend who lives what he writes and is a source of joy in my life. I would rather go to lunch with him than almost anyone else!

And it gives me outrageous delight to dedicate my part of this book to Jane and our son, Justin, who was conceived and born during the writing process. My hope and prayer are that he will have a passion to reach his own generation with the reckless hope of Christ.

David: I was a seven-year-old in vacation Bible school when I became a believer. In the twenty-four years since then, I have been exposed to the full gamut of evangelicalism. I went to Christian school for eight years, stayed active in church and parachurch ministries throughout ten years of college and graduate school, and married a delightful Christian woman.

The truth is that I have never doubted the faith. Despite attacks and disappointments, I have never really doubted that Jesus is who he said he is. I have never really doubted that God is real and cares about us. But as I got older in my faith, I began to see Christian brothers and sisters falling away, I saw the world become seemingly more fractured, and I saw painfully little change in my own heart. I began to feel a sense of despair.

The despair deepened as my job as a psychologist brought me face to face with unthinkable evil on a daily basis. Nearly every day I listened as children told me their stories, many of which are too horrific to recount here. I began to think, "Is there any hope for them? Is there any hope for this world?" At times it almost seemed better to not grant myself too much hope, for fear of being disappointed again. I still believed that God is good and powerful but I realized that I was not convinced things were going to get much better. I realized that I had quietly adopted the almost fatalistic view that the world was on an unalterable course toward its final doom.

The turning point, frankly, was this book. When Todd and I began talking about this project, I realized that we had some unique things to offer. There have already been dozens of articles and a handful of books written about this generation, some even from a Christian perspective. We realized that we had two distinctives, however. First, we were both members of the generation. Most of the other books were written by older authors who were observing the generation from the outside. We realized that we could write from within.

Second, we noticed that nearly all of the Christian writings seemed to boil down to marketing the church to the generation. The focus was clearly on understanding the generation in order to tailor programs to suit it. We could find nothing that outlined a comprehensive theology for the generation. It was here that not only did we find our second distinctive, but also where I rediscovered my own hope.

I had become so focused on the daily barrage of bad news in the newspaper and in my office that I had almost lost sight of what God was doing in the world. I needed the perspective that Scripture provides. Todd took the lead in laying out a theology that clearly illustrates that God is in the business of putting a broken world back together. Our God has been in this business throughout history, he has promised to continue it until perfection in the future, and he is at work doing it right now.

Sometimes I lack the perspective to see that God is at work in my life or in the lives of those around me. Sometimes I fail to see how God could be in command of a world that seems to be spinning out of control. The reality is, however, that he is still at work bringing it all together.

The good news of this book is that God can be trusted to be good. He has a commitment to us from which he will never waver. Because we can count on these things to be true, we have hope.

I am grateful to my wife, Ellen, who helped us achieve continuity between our two discrepant writing styles through her insightful edits. She also provided the graphs in the first chapter. Every day I am amazed that I have the privilege to be married to such a talented, loving, fun, and wonderful woman.

I am also grateful to the pastoral staff at the Church at Charlotte, especially Jim Kallam and Mark Hoffman. They have modeled for me what it looks like to live out the Christian faith with integrity and authenticity.

I am grateful to Mark and Joan Mauriello for the interest they have taken in me and this project. Their extraordinary children, Mary Beth, Cliff, and Michael, serve as living tributes to their dedication to both God and family.

I am grateful to be blessed by an incredible family. My parents, Herb and Ann, and my brother, Brian, have shaped me into the person that I am today. Likewise, friends like Todd Williams, Scott Vermillion, Randy Borum, and others have molded me in remarkable ways.

I am grateful for the experience of being able to write with my dear friend and brother, Todd Hahn. He is not only one of the smartest people I have ever known, but he is a man of great character. He's also hysterically funny.

Finally it is with great joy that I dedicate this book to my grandmother, Muriel Peebles. Without her financial and emotional support, I would never have made it through graduate school. Throughout my entire life she has been the quiet, humble, and wise cornerstone of my wonderful family. She is a dear treasure to me.

PART
1

DESCRIPTION

Meet the Generation

Talking 'bout Our Generation

There is something deeply troubling about what is happening to our generation. In the midst of all the analysis and intergenerational bickering, there is the reality that we have become the first completely post-Christian generation in the history of our culture. Our generation does not know God. Yet this is a generation that yearns and searches for spiritual reality. So far it is not finding it in the church.

The church has sensed the need to respond effectively to this complex and resistant group, yet it has been unable to do so thus far. Our generation avoids the organized church like no other before it. The church has tried to understand the generation and appeal to it with services featuring skits, flashing multimedia, and upbeat music, but it still stays away.

What is missing is a deeper understanding of the generation's core issues and a clearly articulated theology that speaks truth to a group of people who are not sure that truth exists anymore.

First, we need to cover some familiar territory and discuss the characteristics of the generation. It will become evident that these characteristics, while not true of each individual member of the generation, are largely true for believers and nonbelievers alike. This peek into the psyche of our generation will be a view from within.

In Search of a Defining Term

From *Happy Days* to hippies, previous generations of young people seemed easy to describe. There were a familiar look and a commonly accepted set of values and behaviors. This generation is different. One writer says this generation is "a myth—an imaginary resolution of real contradictions. Many young people do like grunge rock, gourmet coffee, and green politics, at least for the moment. Many do share an ironic immersion in the mass media and an interest in alternatives to it; many are well disposed to political activism, especially if it is cost-free and corporate-sponsored. But these characteristics don't cohere into a shared identity."[1]

We are certainly a generation without any cohesive identity. We seem to have no defining moments or icons. As a result we are difficult to sum up in a single term. This frustrates the writers and other thinkers who like to coin phrases that capture the nature of a group of people or a time in history. Just think of the "Baby Boomers" or the "Me Decade" to remind yourself of our desire to hang a single label on a group or a time.

One member of this generation writes, "We are a culture, a demographic, an outlook, a style, an economy, a scene, a political ideology, an aesthetic, an age, a decade, and a literature."[2] Can we really be all of these things?

Because this generation has been so difficult to characterize, each writer seems to feel the pressure to be the one to come up with the defining term. The offerings include "Generation X," "The Blank Generation," "The 13th Generation," "The New Lost Generation," "The MTV Generation," and "The Repair Generation." Even the silly term "yiffies" (which stands for young, individualistic, freedom-minded, and few) has slipped into the literature. This term is not only inane but incorrect. The commonly accepted notion that the generation is relatively small—which is how some account for its lack of respect from advertisers and others—is a myth. In fact, it is the second largest generation in U.S. history.

Each of these terms, with the obvious exception of the last, is a viable option for the generation's defining label. Many prefer "Generation X," but we have opted for the term "Baby Busters."

Baby Busters logically follow the Baby Boomers. Some have suggested, though, that the label is an insult to the generation, as if to suggest that a "boom" was followed by a "bust," a big disappointment or flop. Others object to it because it seems to define the generation solely by contrasting it with another generation. Some find this particularly distasteful because of the conflict and hostility felt between the two generations.

Surprisingly, however, most of the opposition to the label comes from those outside the generation. Older observers are the ones writing the articles that decry the use of the term. It is as if the generation itself is so diverse and uninterested in such matters that it could scarcely care. Ask nearly any Buster what label he or she prefers and you will likely get the response that has almost become a motto for the generation, "whatever." So, with this said, "Baby Busters" will serve as our term of choice.

Defining the Generation by Its Approach to Life

Throughout most of history, demographic models have defined generations. Birth rates were the principle means of establishing cut-off points to separate one generation from another. This is why we typically hear that the Baby Buster generation began in 1965 and seems to have continued through the mid-1980s.

However, in their book, *13th Generation,* Howe and Strauss make a compelling argument that we would understand this cohort better by considering its approach to life, as opposed to purely demographic trends. Using this model they argue that the generation began with those born in 1961, because their attitudes about life are closer to those of the rest of the Busters than they are to those of the Boomers. Although this cut-off is entirely subjective, it appears to be more useful than the pure demographic model.

Regardless of the exact date it began, the more important point to remember is that we understand the generation best by its defining characteristics and approach to life and not merely by demographics.

Characteristics of the Generation

Despite the bashing this generation has suffered for its transgressions and flaws, there is good within it.

Despite its diversity, we identify some common traits. And despite its lack of cohesion and identity, a sense of character emerges.

The following characteristics and descriptions—both good and bad—are obviously not true of every Baby Buster. They are not meant to stereotype. The descriptors merely represent what is generally true and characteristic of the whole group. Individually the authors do not have some of the same experiences or attitudes that characterize the rest; however, because we identify ourselves as Baby Busters, we will own these characteristics for ourselves as we discuss our generation.

Negative Characteristics

We Are Hopeless

A college student walks across campus with a button on his shirt that reads, "Since I gave up hope, I feel much better." It is unlikely that any phrase could describe the attitude of this generation better. Busters are, in many ways, nearly without hope. It is not necessarily a kind of despair that says life is not worth living but, rather, a sense that despite one's best efforts, the world may not get much better.

These beliefs are not completely unfounded. It is the first generation in this century that will not meet or surpass our parents' standard of living. It is the most aborted, neglected, and abused generation in history. It grew up witness to the aftermath of the collapse of the previous generation's hopes.

The Boomers hoped in the power of government to create a just society. This collapsed with Vietnam, Watergate, Iran-Contra, and the S&L bailouts. The Boomers hoped in the challenging of conventional mores that would allow for more individual freedom and liberty. This collapsed with AIDS and the emotional fallout of the sexual revolution. All the hopes of the Boomers came crashing down on the Busters. Actor Michael J. Fox, himself a Buster, said in a recent interview, "I think there is a lot of resentment among my generation toward the Baby Boomers. They got 'free love'; we got AIDS. They got acid trips; we got crack. People graduate from college and work at McDonald's. It's a different world." Another writer puts it this way: "One characteristic of [Baby Busters] is already crystal clear: They resent Baby Boomers. In the eyes of the young adults, Boomers had a party and didn't clean up the mess."[3]

In their prime, Boomers believed that they could change the world. Busters have no such hope. The hopes of the previous generations seem empty or, at least, inaccessible to us. For example, our parents could hope to be financially secure enough to buy a house and support a family by the time they were thirty. For most of this younger generation, this is not a viable option. The Ameri-

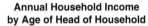

**Annual Household Income
by Age of Head of Household**

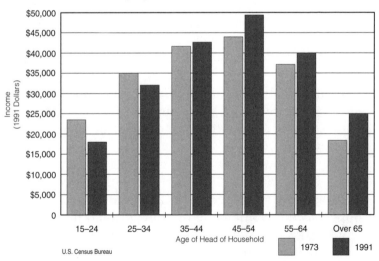

Description

can Dream, as defined by earlier generations, is a foreign concept to most Busters.

The sense of hopelessness extends beyond measurable declines, however. At the core it springs from the realization that nothing helps. Nothing can make the world better. Nothing can keep us from destroying ourselves. Nothing—not government, not religion, not science, not anything!

The lack of hope is the hallmark of this generation. All the other negative characteristics of the generation—living for the immediate thrill, feeling disconnected from others, the cynical attitude, the anger—ultimately seem to spring from this central feature.

Even young Christians are infected with this sense of hopelessness. The personal change promised and expected to be part of the territory of faith is slow to happen, if it ever does. For many every time a high-profile spiritual leader falls, it serves to haunt us with the idea that perhaps real change is an illusion.

The unity of believers for which so many of us hope and pray also seems unattainable, especially in view of how the Christian community often appears even more fragmented than the culture in which it exists. We are embarrassed by the hypocrisy and backbiting and divisiveness that seem typical of many who call themselves Christians. At times we seem to have nothing to offer the world except what they already have: a lack of integrity and discord. Yes, Baby Buster Christians have reasons to feel hopeless too. We don't know what it means to hope in the Lord.

We Are Immediate

What would you do if you looked around and surveyed a world gone out of control and there wasn't much you could do about it? Would you obsess and worry or would

you live for the moment? The Busters have chosen the latter option. Like the stories of parties held in beach houses about to get hit by a hurricane, the Busters are having a blast. The here-and-now thrill seems as meaningful as anything else in life. Whether it's bungee-jumping, impulsive travel, or a craving for more exciting forms of entertainment, the effect is always the same: It makes life fun.

Fun is often the operative word for Busters. Things must be fun to be meaningful. Things must be fun to be worth doing. If a job is not fun, leave it. According to Buster philosophy, it's better to take a temporary "McJob" that permits you flexible hours and more time for personal fun than a high-pressure, demanding job that cuts into these opportunities.

Immediate access to entertainment and information is also characteristic of this generation. Raised on video games, VCRs, and MTV, entertainment of every form has become a core feature of our culture. Busters find and digest facts rapidly. Overwhelming amounts of information are available to anyone linked to a computer network or hooked to a cable system.

Not surprisingly this generation has been criticized for its short attention span. Given their immediate access to nearly all forms of information and amusement, is it any wonder that Busters often seem impatient and restless? We soak up necessary information and then move on to more important matters. This "just the facts, ma'am" approach takes in facts and leaves out the systematic analysis. We prefer to draw our own conclusions.

Christian members of this generation are immediate as well. Bible studies and sermons must skip deeper understandings and be relevant, speaking only to felt needs. God should answer prayers in haste. Things must make sense now. Programs must be fun. We don't know what it means to wait on the Lord.

We Are Disconnected

This is the therapeutic generation. While growing up, young Busters were often hauled off to therapy and counseling sessions. Yet despite this therapeutic culture, there seems to have never been a group so out of touch with itself—and with others. In many important ways we are disconnected from deep relationships: relationships with others, relationships with ourselves, and even relationship with our God.

This is a generation that feels disconnected and out of step with the larger culture. One of the characters in Douglas Coupland's *Generation X* describes this eloquently when he says, "We live small lives on the periphery; we are marginalized and there's a great deal in which we choose not to participate. We wanted silence and we have that silence now."[4] This marginalized, silent existence has left Busters isolated and at odds with others. Filled with resentment for being cut out of the good life by society's elders, this generation has not only been shoved to the periphery but has, in many cases, willingly moved out of the mainstream of the culture. We feel denied access to opportunities while being criticized for our lack of achievement. No wonder there is much in our culture in which we still choose not to participate.

The sense of being disconnected extends to our experience of being cut off from significant relationships as well. Busters have reaped the consequences of the selfishness of parents, who, convinced that the highest good was self-discovery and self-fulfillment, chose divorce in record numbers. And for many divorce was nearly the least of their worries. The rates of abuse, neglect, and abandonment skyrocketed when we were kids. As a result, this generation grew up disconnected from our families. All that comes with an intact family—a sense of security, a sense of belonging, a place to be socialized and learn values, a place to enjoy emotional warmth, a place to be cared for—was lost to Baby Busters. Because the family is so central to not only socialization, but the healthy development and understanding of emotions, this generation became disconnected from ourselves as well as from others.

Is it any wonder that these factors—the sense of being denied access to opportunity and the disintegration of the family—have combined to create such a disconnected generation? Even Christians, particularly those who have experienced divorce or who have been abused, feel disconnected from God. How can you trust someone called Father if you were abandoned by the only other father you have ever known? How can the family

Number of Divorces, 1950–1985 and the Number of Children Involved

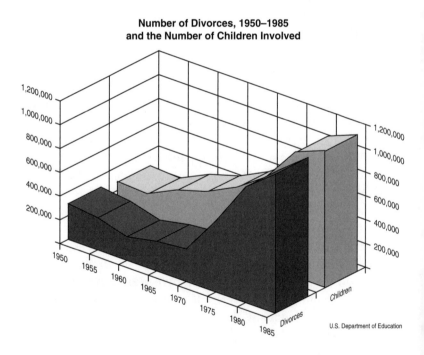

U.S. Department of Education

Description

of God minister to you when your sense of family is so distorted? We don't know what it means to know God as a loving Father.

We Are Cynical

To many, the cynicism of the generation is its most striking feature. These themes show up repeatedly in the literature. George Barna writes, "Busters are world-class skeptics, cynical about mankind and pessimistic about the future."[5] Another writer concludes that "as a group, these individuals tend to be more cynical"[6] than those of previous generations. Many Busters readily admit that we are a disillusioned group of people. As a generation we have learned not to believe anyone or anything that promises too much. The chance of disappointment is too great, so we defend against being hurt by false hopes and empty promises.

As a generation we are cynical not only because we have had our hopes deflated, but because we have learned not to trust anything that offers firm, absolute answers. Most Busters are deeply cynical of those who claim to know the answers to life's problems. Consequently the Christian faith is viewed with suspicion. If Christianity has all the answers, why hasn't it solved all the problems? Christians can't even get their own house in order, some observe.

Even Christians of this generation have felt the compulsion to be cynical. We sometimes listen to the pastor with suspicion. Is he having an affair while he tells us to keep ourselves pure? Is he going to say God told him something in an attempt to lighten my wallet? We often view testimonies as dubious and suspect. We question if real change can ever occur.

Christians of this generation have become as cautious and cynical as our unbelieving peers. Lodged somewhere deep within us is the strong fear that God has turned his back on us because of our repugnant culture. Perhaps we can no longer count on God's intervention. Perhaps we crossed the line as a society and cannot be certain that God will be good to us any longer. We have nearly come to the point where we accept these things as true and have become cynical of anyone who holds out hope for us. We have nearly come to the point of doubting that God is powerful and in control. We feel we must take matters into our own hands. We don't really know if God is truly good. We don't know what it means to trust God.

We Are Angry

Gruesome accounts of the violence perpetrated by our generation fill our newspapers and TV reports. It seems that there has never before been a group of young people so filled with anger and hatred and so lacking in remorse. The reality is, however, that all of us have become weary of these accounts. We know them all too well and need no new retellings to convince us that this is a generation of angry young men and women. We see it in the violence. We see it in the passive-aggressive "laziness." We see it in the biting sarcasm, the preferred mode of humor for most Busters. This is a generation of individuals who feel left out and angry. This is a generation that has been abused—often in very real ways—and burns with hate.

The Baby Busters pour out their wrath most often on the Baby Boomers. The Busters fault the Boomers not just for ripping up the culture but also for criticizing those who came after them for not straightening it out well enough. For many, Boomers personify hypocrisy and are not worthy of respect.

The anger goes beyond just generational discontent, however, and seems to emanate from the deeper sense of hopelessness and despair. Indeed the lack of hope has

Description

not only spilled out in the form of reckless thrill seeking but also as violence born of anger and frustration.

The Christians of this generation have had a taste of anger as well. We are angry at this chaotic world for its sin, angry at each other for our divisiveness, angry at ourselves for our weakness, angry at God for his failure to intervene. Yet this is not all righteous anger but often an anger that grows out of frustration. The reason our frustration gives way to these intensely angry feelings is that we, like the rest of the world, still lack hope that things will ever really change. We don't know what it means to be at peace with ourselves, with others, or with our God.

Positive Characteristics

We Are Realistic

After reading the past few pages, you undoubtedly understand why Howe and Strauss call us "a generation with a PR problem."[7] Yet despite all this gloom and doom, healthy features abound.

Some of our positive characteristics are the flip side of the negative characteristics. For example, current circumstances may have left us as a generation without much hope but they have also left us with healthy pragmatism and realism.

We tend to have realistic expectations for ourselves and for others. We know that people are fallible and have their limits. We know that it is as easy for us to fail someone as it is for us to be failed.

We understand the truth of the old phrase that there is no such thing as a free lunch. Our realistic view of the world tells us that there are no easy answers. We must work hard to pay our own way and to make a difference in the world.

Some say that members of this generation would rather help an old lady across the street than lobby for senior citizens' rights. This seems to be a fair assessment. Because of our realistic approach to life, we tend to avoid unmanageable concerns and focus on issues that can be solved at the grassroots level. For example, taking care of the environment is an example of a big issue that can be addressed successfully by individuals and local communities—everyone can recycle. There is a strongly held belief that each individual can make a difference if he or she chooses.

This generation approaches other issues, such as homelessness, date rape, drug abuse, and AIDS, in ways that make them manageable. There are no illusions that these problems can be solved entirely. The objective is no longer to change the world but to make a difference. Despite the shift to the fringes of society, this is a collective of individuals who want to make a difference in the lives of others around them.

We Are Adaptive

Witness a world gone mad and you have very few options. You could live in a cave, jump off a bridge, or learn to adapt. Most Busters have learned to adapt. We perceive that things are falling apart and we have decided to face the situation squarely, while we strive to make it all work.

Baby Busters often come up with creative, innovative solutions to the problems that face them, but as Barna argues, "The key skill is not innovation but adaptation."[8] Life used to be more clearly defined, but we now live in an ambiguous world that is constantly changing. As a result we have learned to adapt to novel circumstances and demands.

The same forces that lead us to become disconnected from others have also created in us an ability to move in and out of situations and relationships with relative ease. As a whole we have developed skills that allow us to be flexible and to quickly adapt to a variety of circumstances.

We tend to be able to do many different things well. We are able to relate to others who are different from ourselves better than any other generation before us. We have also equipped ourselves with a large arsenal of professional and semiprofessional skills that enable us to survive economically. In these ways most of us possess a broad base of abilities that can help us succeed.

Most Busters would consider themselves to be survivors. We have learned how to adapt so we can survive. Howe and Strauss write, "As a group, they aren't what older people wish they were, but rather what they themselves know they need to be: street smart survivalists clued into the game of life the way it really gets played, searching for simple things that work in a cumbersome society that offers little to them."[9] Yes, we have learned how to adapt to the game of life, even when the rules are constantly changing.

We Are Resourceful

Despite treatment that we perceive as unfair, this is not a generation of victims. As a whole we tend to reject the "politically correct" attempts to cast every underdog as a helpless victim. The Third Millennium Declaration, a manifesto written by a group of Busters from many different backgrounds, derides "impotent left-wing dogma" that has created "a society of victims and dependents."

This generation, by contrast, is a collection of individuals who are resourceful and tenacious. We pull ourselves up by the proverbial bootstraps, even when we feel cheated and blamed. Corporately we feel robbed, yet individually we drive hard to succeed in spite of this.

In our drive to make it, we have learned how to draw from our resources, both internal and external. Collectively our internal resources tend to be our adaptability, our innovation, our toughmindedness, and our persistence. A poll by the Barna Research Group found that a full 94 percent of Busters considered themselves to be "hard workers." This underscores the following realities. We do not believe things in life will be offered freely to us and we are fully willing to work hard to achieve our goals.

We are also a generation that has used humor to great advantage as not only a means of expression but also as a means of persuasion. The styles range from the heavily sarcastic to the quirky and bizarre. In each instance, though, Busters are able to communicate quickly and effectively through humor.

As we have discussed, being an immediate generation does have its disadvantages. On the other hand, having

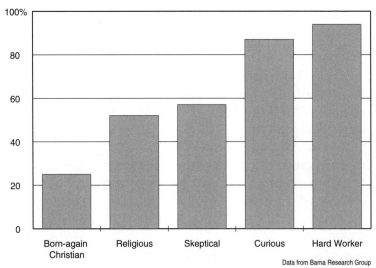

Key Adjectives
Busters Use to Describe Themselves

Data from Barna Research Group

Description

immediate access to information and entertainment certainly has many advantages. One of the biggest external resources that we have is technology. In a true sense we have become masters of technology. From computers to cable we use it well. We have millions of facts readily at our disposal, either in our heads or on our hard drives. We take these facts and we integrate them ourselves into meaningful pieces of information.

Busters are also skilled at using others as resources. This is arguably the best generation of all time in networking ability. While we may be disconnected from others in meaningful ways, we appreciate the need to connect with others to accomplish tasks. We have no qualms about crossing such boundaries as race, gender, or organizational and political affiliation to achieve our goals. As we see our culture disintegrate and break into little factions, we understand the need to integrate and to close up divisions.

Our resourcefulness will undoubtedly serve us well as we move through life. We are able to draw on our own innovation, persistence, and humor to survive. At the same time, we use our skills with technology and people networking to help us succeed.

We Are Accepting

You don't need to check out demographic data to know that this is the most diverse generation in history. Not only do we possess tremendous ethnic diversity, but we also come from a wide variety of backgrounds and represent an incredibly mixed bag of lifestyles.

As a result of being exposed to so many differences, we have become a group of individuals who have learned to accept others different from ourselves. We have learned how to get along with others who are dramatically different from us. Differences often threatened previous generations, but we tend to respect and celebrate them. We accept and relate well to those of other races, to those with different belief systems, and to those from different backgrounds. It is not uncommon for us to interact with peers who grew up in nontraditional family configurations or who espouse wildly different political beliefs.

We Christians know the pitfalls of being too accepting of all beliefs and lifestyles. Being accepting of every belief or behavior is not a virtue. Yet being accepting does have its advantages. As a whole it gives us the opportunity to show mercy toward others and to earn the right to have our views considered. It is in this way that the generation's acceptance of others is a positive characteristic.

A Last Look at the Generation

The point of this discussion is not to create stereotypes but to highlight traits that seem to be shaping the emerging character of this generation and to identify some of the core issues with which we wrestle. One writer comments, "In many ways, the baby-bust character has not fully evolved or solidified."[10] While this may be true to some degree, we are seeing it begin to take shape.

It is difficult to sum up a whole generation with a few choice adjectives. We are an incredibly diverse, eclectic generation. We are a group that resents being grouped and stereotyped. In spite of all the diversity, however, a cohesive identity is finally being realized.

Above all, this is a generation in need of hope. It must be a hope that this fractured, disconnected world can be saved. It must be a hope that life has ultimate meaning and purpose. It must be a hope that does not disappoint us.

2

Understand the Generation

Like every generation before it, this is a group whose identity has been shaped and molded by the culture in which it was raised. The forces that were hard at work shaping the society's terrain left their fingerprints all over the Baby Buster generation.

During the formative years of the generation, fundamental changes were occurring in our culture. The core, unifying beliefs of our society were being challenged and discarded. The resulting collapse of institutions—such as the traditional family—coupled with the addition of new stressors—such as AIDS and environmental fears—helped shape the character of the generation. The rapid advances in technology also created some of the Buster personality. All of these factors combined to mold the generation's identity.

A Generation of Whiners?

Imagine opening the *Washington Post* to be greeted by this jarring headline: THE BORING TWENTIES: GROW UP, CRY-BABIES. YOU'RE AMERICA'S LUCKIEST GENERATION. To be sure, this is the view that older generations often have of Baby Busters. We are viewed as a collection of lazy, ungrateful whiners. Columnist Joseph Spear writes, "the thing that bothers me most about them is they think they invented anguish. Nobody ever suffered feelings of alienation before they happened upon the planet. Nobody ever had to endure the ache of broken homes. Nobody ever had to deal with a rotten job market."[1]

He goes on to contrast the petty whines of Baby Busters with the true hardships of previous generations. We whine about not getting a high-paying job right out of college, but his parents lived through the Great Depression, desperate for any job, standing in soup lines, cashing in insurance policies to put food on the table. He worked in the military for a mere $5,000 per year and later took a second-rate job, even with a graduate degree. We whine about our broken families, yet his father left home for war, his uncle died in combat, and many of his friends were killed in Vietnam.

He does make a compelling argument. Why should a generation that is so affluent and has such a relatively easy life be so whiny? Why is this generation so angry and deeply troubled by comparably little hardship? These are both good questions.

The answer to the first question of why this generation is so whiny is that most Baby Busters are, in fact, not whiners at all. Columnists and other members of the media have determined that this is an ungrateful group of crybabies who need to be put in their place. While this is an angry, deeply cynical generation, we are not whiners. Most careful observers of the generation agree that the whiner stereotype does not stack up to reality.

Granted there are occasional high-profile Busters who whine and complain. However, this does not seem to be characteristic of the whole generation. Instead of being a big group of crybabies, we are a tenacious and self-reliant bunch. The notion that Baby Busters are whiners is largely a myth.

A Generation without a Core

The second question of why this generation seems so deeply angered and troubled by comparably little hardship must be answered in context. Spear himself stumbled across part of the answer in the same column. He quoted a distraught young woman who said, "We lack something. We have no core." Spear's contention was that the generation needs to get some perspective and recognize how its plight stacks up against the hardships of previous generations. He may have missed the point. Anyone who thinks that a poor economy is anywhere near the root of the anger and cynicism has oversimplified the problem.

These issues are not created by the temporary setbacks or difficulties that this generation is facing; they go much deeper than that. The anger and cynicism, as well as the sense of hopelessness and disconnectedness, come from the real fact that this generation lacks something. It has no core.

As a generation we have been robbed of something much more significant than a good economy. We have been raised without a sense of truth. We have been taught that all values and ethics are entirely subjective. As a generation of young people, we have been denied a sense of the wonder and glory of God. In short we were raised in a way that has left us as a generation without a core. We have no moral or spiritual connections. We no longer share a system of beliefs as other generations before us have. Instead, each member is left to define truth, morality, and even God as he or she chooses. This has left us disconnected and alone.

The generations that preceded the Baby Boomer generation grew up believing that something must be capable of being proven, even replicated, to be believed. This worldview arose out of the scientific model that focused on rational, empirical ways of knowing. It became the prevailing system of thought for our culture during the decades prior to the 1980s.

This alarmed many Christians because it seemed to leave no room for faith in something—or Someone—that was unseen, unmeasurable, or untestable. There seemed to be no room for the spiritual in the marketplace of ideas. So when the unofficial revolt against the scientific model began, many people of faith rejoiced, believing that they now had a new window of opportunity to approach the culture with the gospel. Unfortunately a more insidious worldview prevailed. In the new system, empiricism was rejected as the only way of knowing and replaced with myriad options. There became multiple paths to knowledge and understanding, none more important or real than another. As a result, spiritual ideas were acceptable, but no system of belief was allowed to be more "true" than another. Thus the focus of concern shifted from the rather straightforward issue of proving the existence of God to the more complex, tangled task of convincing unbelievers that Christianity had an exclusive grasp of ultimate truth. After all, truth was subjective and relative, leaving no option for an objective, absolute system of belief.

The impact of relativism has wormed its way into the church. Take a look at our Bible studies. Many interpretations of the same passage are allowed and accepted as equally valid. Everyone's opinion is considered equally viable. Respecting the ideas of others has been given precedence over a search for the actual intention of the author. In fact the unrealized assumption is that one's sincere ideas are synonymous with truth.

The overwhelming majority of Baby Busters do not believe in absolute truth. We are a generation of individuals who zealously protect the rights of others to express their own opinions. A person's opinion has become their "truth." As a generation without a sense of truth, we have no unifying beliefs. We simply all agree to respectfully disagree.

This concept of truth has shaped the generation's worldview. It has also contributed to its sense of disconnection and fragmentation. Without a set of commonly held core beliefs, we are left as a group of individuals who are alienated from each other. We are left without much in common.

In the introduction to his compilation of significant writings from within the generation, Douglas Rushkoff wrote, "Busters feel liberated from the constraints of ethical systems, but also somewhat cast adrift. It must be nice to have something external to believe in. Something that doesn't move. Something absolute. Having no such permanent icon (no God, no Country, no Superhero) we choose instead—by default actually—to experience life as play, and trust that the closer we come to our own true intentions, the closer we will come to our own best intentions."[2]

Rushkoff nicely captures the shift from seeking external sources of meaning, including God, to internal ones. The few unifying beliefs among the generation center on the conviction that each of us must rely on ourselves to create meaning and purpose out of life. We can create the good life for ourselves, centering on fun and play, and perhaps carve out our own uniquely personal moral and spiritual beliefs along the way. This rugged, self-sufficient individualism continues to persist in the generation. There is a belief among nearly all members of the generation that, though the world may be headed deeper into chaos, they can be successful if they work hard enough.

If this is the shared conviction and the guiding ethic, then is it any wonder that when the generation is met with grim economic and social realities, it becomes angry and cynical? As a generation we feel as if someone has lied to us. We feel tricked. The slackers and others who drop out of mainstream culture represent a rebellion against the perceived lies and tricks.

At the same time, this generation's attitude has been shaped heavily by the disintegration of the family. The dramatic increases in divorce and child abuse are only the most obvious examples of how the family became unglued when our generation was growing up. True, other generations had fathers going off to war and mothers working in shipyards, but the basic fabric of the family remained intact. Children were nurtured and instructed and kept safe, even though times were tough. Our generation was raised by parents who were often experimenting with their own liberation and personal freedoms and, for the first time, saw children as a nuisance or hindrance to self-growth.

As a result, all that comes from being a part of a loving, nurturing family, including the ability to gain perspective, delay gratification, and connect to significant others, was largely lost to the Busters. The disintegration of the family left an unmistakably devastating impact on the generation.

All of these factors conspired together to create a generation that, in effect, has no core. In addition, new and unprecedented stressors appeared that helped intensify the maturing Busters' sense of fear and hopelessness.

Fears That Shaped the Generation

During every year since the birth of the oldest members of the generation, violent crime has increased. Worse yet, violence and the threat of violence have appeared among children in the neighborhoods and in the schools. It is no longer petty schoolyard violence where a couple of punches are thrown. It is guns in bookbags and drive-by shootings. As the youngest members of the generation complete high school, metal detectors at the entrance are no longer uncommon sights.

The stressor of violence has affected the generation in many ways. It has created a sense of unsafety and randomness. Many have responded by indulging in escapism in the reckless forms we have discussed. Others have moved to the fringes of mainstream society. The majority, however, have just lived with the fear.

Environmental fears have also gripped the generation. This is the first generation that has become absolutely convinced that the world is being ripped apart. Many Busters are alarmed that the earth is being robbed and depleted of its sustaining natural resources. This perception of environmental crisis has replaced the worries of nuclear annihilation that troubled the Boomers as children. The concerns range from fears of the damaging effects of pollution and acid rain to indignation that the earth is being mishandled by heartless industry.

These environmental worries, often misunderstood and belittled by older generations, are acutely felt by

Baby Busters. The generation has dealt with these fears head-on, organizing and promoting local efforts to help recycle, plant, and become more environmentally aware. The advocacy of the generation nearly always takes shape at the community level. These grassroots campaigns are a hallmark of Buster involvement. Ours is a generation with no delusions of saving the world but a real desire to save our corner of it.

Other concerns, such as the fear of AIDS, the impact of drugs, and the trauma of divorce, all made the world an unsafe place for Baby Busters. The scars of physical abuse, which showed a four-fold increase in reports during our childhood years, also affected the generation's ability to form close connections with others. Unlike other generations before us, Baby Busters often do not even care to connect and identify with each other.

Generational Confusion

Developmentally Baby Busters are not unlike other generations when they were at the same age. Most people in their teens and twenties are cynical and feel mistreated by their elders. Most people were more impulsive and immediate when they were young. However, Busters are not only unique in our hopeless view of the world at any age when we should be naive and idealistic, but we are also unique in our resistance to being grouped together.

In generations past, young people gladly affiliated with and felt an affinity toward each other. Other generations were made up of a diverse group of individuals too but ultimately they sensed a kinship with each other. To say that a group of young people represented a "generation" was accepted as conventional wisdom.

This is not so with the Baby Busters. Most seem almost to wince at being grouped together. One Buster, when asked what he thought of the term "Generation X," said, "I don't know. I don't see myself as part of any specific social group." He undoubtedly speaks for many in the generation who resist being labeled and stereotyped.

The individualistic focus of the generation is largely responsible for this mindset. Each member has come to see him- or herself as intensely different from others. Without a shared system of belief, this is actually true. There is little to connect the members of the generation. We may rally together around issues of concern, but there is no longer a common creed. In many ways Baby Busters mirror the large society in which we were raised. The culture, like us, is no longer unified but has instead become fragmented into millions of individual pieces. This fact, as we shall see, has much to do with why the church has missed the Baby Busters.

In short, this so-called Generation X is not a group of apathetic whiners. Instead this is a group that has been robbed of something; it lacks a core. It has been taught that there are no absolutes and that you must look inside to determine what is right and true. This, coupled with the introduction of new fears and stressors, has created a generation that is more than "somewhat cast adrift." It is a fragmented generation of individuals drifting apart in an increasingly divided culture.

3

How Christians
Missed the Generation

Christianity and Culture Reconsidered

The surveys and statistics tell us that Baby Busters are not much interested in the institutional church. Compared to other generations at the same age, a disproportionate number of Busters are actively avoiding the traditional Christian faith. At the same time, there is every indication that this is a strongly spiritually minded group. According to Barna, nearly two-thirds say that having a close relationship with God is very important, yet only one quarter would describe themselves as "born-again Christians," and a little more than a third say that being involved in any kind of local church is important.

Somehow the church has failed to make a connection. How could this happen?

Christians have a long history of being the dominant molders of tradition and ethics in our society. It used to be that nearly everyone understood, at some level, that Judeo-Christian values were the underpinnings of our culture. Individuals understood and operated from this premise, whether or not they personally endorsed the matching religious beliefs. These ideas seemed to be woven into the fabric of the society.

This fabric remained relatively intact for over a century and a half. However, it began to unravel about thirty years ago. In the 1960s and early 1970s, such landmark events as the Vietnam War, the Kennedy and King assassinations, and Watergate ripped a hole in the culture from which we have never recovered. These events created a climate in which authority was challenged and suspect, right could not be easily distinguished from wrong, and it was every man for himself. No wonder the rest of the 1970s was labeled the "Me Decade." It was even less surprising that this was followed by the "Greed Decade" of the 1980s. It seems to be the logical progression. Michael Douglas's character in *Wall Street* was not the only one who believed that "Greed is good." As a society we believed it too.

By the end of the 1980s, the stock market had crashed, the junk bond kings and the greedy TV evangelists were in jail, and we were left with our heads spinning. By the 1990s we had no idea what we stood for as a society. We knew greed wasn't so good but we all had our own ideas about what was good. Without a unifying foundation of mutual beliefs, we broke apart into warring factions, each screaming louder than the next for our rights. We became a society of special interest groups, each dedicated to its own agenda. Feminists, homosexuals, ethnic groups, the hearing-impaired, the physically handicapped, and many others became their own persecuted minority bent on coaxing or coercing the rest to give them respect and resources.

Unfortunately Christians followed suit. Instead of being the one group that could bring the unifying message to the culture, we became one of many loudmouthed special interest groups. We tried grasping political power throughout the 80s and into the 90s; we organized boycotts; we protested. At the same time, the liberal branch of the church became even more limp toward truth, excusing—even promoting—the most abhorrent behaviors. Does any of this sound like a group that would be attractive to outside observers?

Even today the modern church continues to act as a special interest faction in an increasingly fragmented world. We have become perceived as a hostile group attempting to impose its agenda on others. It is far from the true nature and purpose of the church.

Out with the Old Worldview

The problem runs deeper than merely being lumped in with the rest of the splinter groups, however. The church is now being actively resisted by the dominant culture. The church is not just perceived as one of many groups that is pushing its agenda. It is seen as being, at best, an outdated dinosaur of an institution and, at worst, a mean-spirited, closed-minded hate group. For many it has become a thing to avoid, even oppose.

As our culture's old worldview of rational empiricism gave way to postmodern thinking, the emphasis shifted to more subjective ways of knowing and understanding. Truth was no longer objective but became viewed as a matter for each individual to determine. Everyone was

Description

entitled to his or her own opinion, and any effort to suggest that one opinion on any issue was more truthful than another was seen as the ugliest of attitudes. Sincerity, on the other hand, became the highest of virtues. It did not matter what you believed, as long as you were sincere. And no one had the right to tell you otherwise!

When the church, with its claim of an exclusive hold on truth, confronted moral issues, it suddenly met with profound resistance in a way that it had not encountered in recent memory. Even when the populace agreed with the church on certain issues, most had been shaped by the postmodern thinking to the extent that they could only respond at a visceral level and not affirm matters of truth. A person's lifestyle choice or behavior could be called "sick" or "weird" but not "wrong" by any objective standard. One only has to watch a few hours of talk shows to be convinced of this.

Christians, however, still hold to certain truths as absolute and, as a result, have become out of step with the culture. When Christians attempt to affirm or advocate these truths, they are counterpunched with charges of being bigoted and mean-spirited. To say that certain lifestyles or behaviors are "sinful" is to be horribly insulting.

The Christian faith was not designed to be received favorably by the cultural elite. Being confronted with one's sinfulness is not something that humans tend to enjoy. Christianity is, inescapably, a scandal, a stumbling block to most. It will always remain so. The important issue to understand, then, is not that we must develop a way to soft-pedal truth to the culture, but that we must recognize that a fundamental shift has taken place. We can no longer count on the culture to operate from a set of principles and standards rooted in the Judeo-Christian ethic. Our culture is no longer passively compliant with the Christian worldview but actively hostile toward it.

The Crisis in Christianity

The modern church has, for the first time in the history of our culture, lost its footing as the principle architect of society's moral structure. No one looks to us for answers to the biggest questions facing our communities any more. As a result of being deposed of this position, we have fought clumsily to regain our former status. In our efforts we seem to have lost our way.

When an organization begins to lose its way, one of the first signs of trouble is a shift in focus away from the larger issues and toward smaller, more manageable goals. In companies, managers begin writing memos about the copying machine while neglecting the strategies for improving efficiency or morale. Supervisors become hypervigilant about missing signatures while failing to initiate ways to improve the company's product, and so on. One company reported seeing its director out on the front lawn of the building picking up small pieces of litter during the same week that a crisis threatened the organization's very existence.

This preoccupation with minutia occurs when the leaders, and subsequently the rank and file, become overwhelmed and lose a sense of direction and purpose. As time goes on, the mission statement that was initially clearly in view becomes obscured by the complexity of the challenges and the sheer enormity of the workload. When overwhelmed, the sense of direction becomes lost, and the concrete, more easily defined tasks take center stage. This gives a false sense of accomplishment in the face of the organization's floundering.

The same is true with the Christian evangelical movement. As a whole we have lost sight of our mission statement. We have become overwhelmed by the complexity and enormity of our charge, so we have opted to pour our efforts into smaller, intensely fought battles. We rage against the evils of abortion, homosexuality, the liberal-biased media, and the humanistic educators. We scream as loudly as our detractors in attempts to hold back the flood of immorality that threatens our culture. Somehow all the shouting and boycotting seem to make us feel as if we are getting somewhere.

The problem is not that these are unimportant issues but rather that they have become our defining issues. The copier is important to a business, but the focus on its misuse should not become consuming; signatures on documents can be vitally important, but they are not paramount. Christians simply cannot afford to be litter-pickers when the house is burning down.

We should never fail to be salt and light in the culture but we do not accomplish this primarily by becoming another factionalized pressure group. The fact that we have become reduced to this suggests that we have been blown off course.

Reclaiming the Mission Statement

When any organization loses its way, it must return to its mission statement. It must rediscover its main purpose for being. The Christian evangelical movement is at that point. We must return to what we hold to be our foundation and purpose.

What is the bottom line for us as Christians? What is our mission statement? Is it to save souls? Is it to promote justice and mercy? Is it to care for the needy? Is it to stand for what is right and moral? Each of these has been suggested or implied by fellow believers to be the primary function of the church.

We argue that the mission statement for the church is to give honor and glory to God. All of these other ideas are subsets of this central premise. This is a simple but profound idea. If kept clearly in mind, it would serve to guide us more than we might imagine.

This simple mission statement provides guidance but it does not give us a comprehensive guide to reaching this generation. Many will find this frustrating. They want a step-by-step plan. They want to be told what to do and how to do it. Unfortunately God does not seem to work like that with the complex issues of life.

We yearn to be told what to do. Let God give us the checklist, and we'll be on our way. This desire has fostered a Bible-as-road-map-for-life model. A recent drama on a Christian radio station had a son puzzling over what his college major should be. His mother suggested that they read the Bible together to find out. What followed was a discussion of how the Bible is relevant to any of life's major decisions. Interestingly they never did discover his major in the pages of Scripture. That issue was dropped by the end of the skit. The message often given is that the solutions to all of life's problems and puzzling questions are buried somewhere in the pages of Scripture, but this is clearly not always the case.

We affirm that the Bible is truly God's word to us. It is relevant and true. It should inform us in the way we should live, but it does not speak to every specific situation we must face. We must always live in the tension of having to make decisions in which there is no obvious right answer, often having to choose between two good and noble options. Should a man take a job in ministry that would mean uprooting his family and leaving his church and community? Should a student quit a fraternity in which he has healthy relationships with nonbelievers to devote more time to a fellowship organization that wants him in leadership? Who knows?

The problem with believing the Bible is a road map for all of life is that we come to pretend we do know what the right answer is in every instance—and if we don't know, give us a few minutes with a Bible concordance, and we'll get right back to you.

The purpose of Scripture is to let us see the heart and character of God so we will be able to love and honor him. Certainly the Bible gives us some moral instruction and guidance, but if we go to its pages focusing on ourselves and our decisions, as if it were a horoscope or an advice column, we miss the point.

The Bible shows us God's heart; it shows us how much he loves us, how much he cares for us, how he yearns for us to know him, how much he hates the things that hurt us or that steal from his glory. The Bible shows us God's character. It shows us that he is pure, blinding love, full of mercy and justice, completely holy and righteous. The Bible gives us a glimpse of God so that we may give him glory and honor with our lives. This is the true purpose of Scripture and the mission statement of the church.

Protest the Protest

With the mission statement firmly in mind, we must critically examine some of the current strategies and tactics that Christians are taking to effect change in this culture and reach this generation. Some approaches appear on the surface to be appropriate and effective, but a closer analysis might suggest that they are misguided.

As we have already discussed, one tactic that evangelicals have taken in recent years is to become a pressure group. If we don't like it, we will protest it, boycott it, denounce it. You name it. We stack the meetings, line the streets, sign the petitions, and so on.

There are at least two major reasons why this approach is off track. First, we will never achieve true spiritual and moral change by social and political means. This approach wrongly suggests that righteousness can be achieved by force and not by a working of God's Spirit. The notion that we can bring about righteousness by influencing or seizing institutions, such as the schools or government, is false and should be completely abandoned. True revival is always a movement of God. It always starts by prayer and repentance and not social action.

A second error with this approach is that it is the same tactic the rest of the special interest groups in the culture use, and it fails to make us distinct in any way, except that we become perceived as hostile and hate-filled. It makes nonbelievers out to be the enemy. We must never lose sight of the fact that nonbelievers are tangled in sin, blinded to what is truly right. They are prisoners of the true Enemy. Any approach that attacks, rather than rescues, them should be reconsidered.

A recent example of how the pressure strategies have failed came when Christians in different parts of the country mobilized to protest a new television series promoted as being particularly violent and vulgar. They sent a signed petition to the network, organized pickets at local TV stations, and contacted potential advertisers about their intentions to boycott any product that sponsored the show. Some local affiliates did pull the show off their lineup, which was regarded as a huge victory by the protesters and reinforced the idea that protests are necessary and effective. Several newspaper articles covered the story, including quotes from protest organizers and reactions from others in the community. Common responses to the protesters were statements like, "Don't these people have anything better to do with their time?" After all the furor died down, the show not only remained on the air and won several major awards but stayed consistently in the top of the ratings. Though the protest won several battles, it lost the war—not because the show remained on the air but because the protest had further alienated Christians from others.

Christians are not called to be a pressure group, forcefully pushing our agenda on the culture, even when we are right. When we choose to become such a group, we do not allow God to be God. We need to honor God by allowing him to demonstrate his power, not by choosing tactics that are the same as those of the special interest groups. Choosing such tactics only serves to alienate us from nonbelievers, shutting off the opportunities to reach them with God's great news. The idea of protesting still appeals to many, however, because it creates bogeymen outside of our ranks and never forces us to look at ourselves. The church needs to look at itself and repent, and then we will have revival.

As members of this generation we must commit ourselves to drawing our peers into relationship with Jesus. We must resist the strong urgings to participate in the pressure group movement. We must reject the isolationist tendencies of many of our spiritual brothers and sisters. Instead we must go boldly into the dark and draw those who are stranded there into the light.

The Triumph of Form over Substance

As Christian leaders have found the church losing ground in attempts to reach this nonbelieving generation, they have developed another strategy that seems highly appealing at first glance. They have learned how to market the church. If nothing else, our culture excels in its ability to market. Advertisers have found out how to create a burning need within us for the most trivial of products. Having observed the tactics used to create such need, we have adopted this as a strategy to "sell" the church. In many cases we have been very successful—at least in some regards. Some churches have exploded, with thousands of members and dozens of specialty programs.

Most attempts to market the church have the same elements as the advertising strategies. First, discover who your audience is. Collect as much demographic information as you possibly can. Second, determine what your audience wants. What are their "felt needs"? Do they feel the need for security or happiness or meaning and purpose? Find out what they want out of life. Then you can construct a message that speaks to those needs, suggesting that the product will meet the needs—at least partially. Third, present the message in a way that is memorable and catches their attention.

The good news about this strategy is that it works. It attracts attention, and it gets a response. The bad news is that it is full of deep pitfalls. The obvious pitfall is that it allows a corrupt culture to dictate what it wants to hear. Who wants to hear about one's own sin? Please tell me practical tips for living instead. Tell me how to manage my time, how to conquer my poor self-esteem, how to communicate better with my kids. Use the Bible if you want, just make it practical and relevant. When the consumer is king, you give the king what he wants.

It might be difficult for some to make an important distinction here. The concern is not marketing. All churches market themselves to some extent. The concern is not about being relevant and contextual. Paul, the founding father of the church, was relevant and contextual. He changed his tactics and style from culture to culture. Some of the best churches today market themselves well and present a wide array of ministries that speak both relevantly and contextually to their congregations. Willow Creek Community Church outside of Chicago is a terrific model of a church that draws non-believers into the church and produces true followers of Christ. There are dozens—perhaps even hundreds—of examples of such churches today.

The concern raised here has more to do with churches that market themselves with little regard for their message. The churches that neglect preaching the central tenets of the faith for fear of offending or driving people away are the real culprits. These are the churches that celebrate form over substance. Certainly many churches are busting at the seams today but only because they have marketed themselves well. They are filled with people who know nothing of repentance and who have no desire to honor God with every part of their lives.

Surprisingly most of the growth in these churches does not come from attracting new believers from the Baby Buster generation but by the migration of members from other churches. It is not the unchurched who are causing the pews to fill up; it is believers from other, usually smaller, churches who are shopping for a better package deal. Busters are, for the most part, not interested.

The reason why this approach is not reaching our generation is because we are keenly attuned to marketing strategy. We recognize better than any previous generation the strategies and tactics people use to sell us their products. For us, the purpose of a slick worship service with all its upbeat music and humor is merely to make us want to buy the product. To us, most churches are trying to sell something that many of us don't want. We want something authentic and genuine. If we do buy it, we may just modify it and put it together with all the other things we've bought, like the Buster who called a local radio talk show and said, "I'm a born-again Christian. Yeah, I believe that Jesus was the Son of God. But I'm also a practicing Buddhist."

The Christian faith is more than a system of beliefs. It is a lifestyle. We tell the truth to others to help them make a lifestyle choice. More importantly we tell the truth to others to allow them to make choices that will bring honor and glory to God.

To Tell the Truth

Some Christian thinkers, in their effort to make the church more "successful" with this resistant group, have argued that attempts to reach this generation with a message claiming to be truth will be lost on us. They claim that the best approach is to make the Christian faith more appealing and interesting instead. Although we, as a generation, have come to embrace the idea of subjective reality, Christians must understand that our faith is ultimately based on truth. When modernity with all its rationality and emphasis on the empirical became the dominant worldview, Christians made the error of chasing the culture by focusing our efforts on trying to "prove" the faith. We brushed up on our apologetics and developed our carefully reasoned arguments. Over time this focus put the church sadly out of step with the current generation. Now in the postmodern era, we are on the brink of making the opposite mistake, which will eventually lead us down a wrong path again. We cannot keep allowing the culture to dictate our message. We must shape the culture, not the other way around.

This generation may believe that most truth is relative, but, frankly, we are not stupid! We have the capacity to understand basic concepts. The generation is not as intellectually frail and feebleminded as some might

Description

suggest. What is needed is an approach that does not abandon concepts of truth but challenges the existing notions. It is a challenging, but reasonable, undertaking to explain to Busters how some "truth" is relative while other truth is absolute. Take, for example, our knowledge of another person. His or her attractiveness may be a relative concept that varies from individual to individual, but that same person's height is not. Height is measured by an objective standard. Other concepts like age and weight are measured by objective standards as well. This is a concept that any person of reasonable intelligence can understand, regardless of the worldview in which he or she has been raised.

The challenge before us is to help other Busters discriminate between objective truth and opinion. Because spiritual concepts lack form, they have been pushed into the realm of opinion by the dominant culture. The reality is, however, that God exists independently of anyone's opinion—in the same way that each of us exists. Have you ever had two friends that you were trying to introduce, but they could never be in the same place at the same time? One of your friends may speculate jokingly that the other person does not exist. Does this opinion now cause your other friend to cease being? Of course not. Your friend is alive, regardless of the feelings or persuasions of anyone else. (And Elvis is dead, regardless of beliefs to the contrary!)

The idea of truth should not be abandoned in an attempt to reach this generation. Instead, effort should be focused on ways to communicate the objective truth of the gospel. Our faith is based on truth and not on opinion. All true believers must eventually come to terms with the exclusive truths that are affirmed in the Christian faith.

There is absolutely nothing wrong with knowing and understanding your audience. There is nothing wrong with being topical and relevant. There is also nothing wrong with using new conventions in worship. But there is something wrong with abandoning the concept of truth and not calling people to a radical commitment to God. When we successfully market our churches while soft-pedaling our message, we might fill up the sanctuary and be glad because people are there to be saved. We must ask ourselves, however: To what kind of faith are we saving them? A faith that does not include a turning away from things that dishonor God and a turning toward God with a desire to honor him with our whole lives is not the Christian faith.

The Need for a New Approach

It is clear that we need to reconsider many of our strategies. Pressure tactics do not effect deep social change. Marketing alone does not yield true disciples. We are at a time when the church must choose well. We can continue in the same direction or we can regroup and move toward something better.

A lot has been written lately about this "new, lost" generation, even from a Christian perspective. Descriptions and prescriptions have flourished. What is lacking, however, is a true theology for Baby Busters.

Recognizing this need we have set out to develop a theology for the generation. In doing so we had two goals in mind. First, we recognized that it must be a theology that is fully informed by and consistent with Scripture. Second, it must be a theology that speaks to the specific and unique needs of this generation yet contains the timeless truths of the Christian faith.

The word *theology* often brings to mind something dull and lifeless, but this should not be the case. Good theology, rooted in truth, should be terrifically compelling. It should speak to the hearts and minds of those who need to hear it. We desired to develop a theology that would stir the generation.

The Story of Our Lifetime

How do we best reach this generation with these compelling truths? We have a message that we want to communicate clearly. To do so we need to choose our medium carefully. For this generation we need to tell a story. In our story we tell of a daring cosmic rescue mission. It is a story of high drama where we join God as the main characters.

All great stories have grand themes: love, betrayal, courage, perseverance. What is the theme of our story? We quickly realize that the central theme for this generation must be hope. We have hope when we come to trust that God is good and in control. This is no small issue. When you have been raised in a world that seems unsafe and out of control, it is hard to have hope. When we draw near to God with a driving passion, we come to believe that he is working things together for good, that he will one day make all things new, and that he will one day wipe every tear away. We have hope because we have come to know God.

If hope is our theme, then what are the elements—the parts—that make up the story? The element of creation is of critical importance to our story. The story must tell how God cares for his creation, including us and the world around us. It must demonstrate clearly how God is even now in the process of restoring his creation. He is not only mending broken lives but bringing all parts of his creation together under his authority.

Baby Busters yearn to be connected not only with the Creator and the creation, but also to others who share the same beliefs and values. Therefore our story must emphasize the element of community. This is, in a sense, the setting of the story as well. It is important for us to know that the story of our lives is somehow woven into the stories of others and theirs into ours.

Despite the desire to move into community, this generation still harbors a deep mistrust of others. Most Busters go to great lengths to create emotional distance for fear of getting hurt or disappointed. Baby Busters must understand that God can be trusted to be good. The element of covenant, then, is important to include in our story. God keeps the promises he makes. It is here, perhaps, where matters of truth are most central. We must be able to count on the promises of God in objective, no uncertain terms. As those living out our stories in the context of a true community, we must also be a reflection of God by being covenant people. We must make and keep our covenants with God and with each other.

Our theology is ultimately a story. It is a story of hope in the midst of brokenness. We live out our story in a world that is broken, in broken relationships, with broken promises. We tell a story where the Creator has become the Repairman. He is sewing together a world that has ripped apart. He is piecing back together shattered relationships. He is making promises that, despite the bleak outlook, he makes good on by the end of the story. He comes through! Like any good story, we don't see how he will make it, but we hope against hope. As we shall see, we have a hope that does not disappoint us.

PART

2

PRESCRIPTION

4

Bringing It All Together

More Than Meets the Eye

Since 1990 when literature on our generation began to pour from the presses, Baby Busters have been analyzed, quantified, and described ad nauseam. Shrewd marketers and television programming executives have mastered the Buster spin—hip, ironic, cynical, yet fun—and have done a fine job of selling everything from cars to cotton clothing to compact discs using the images and language that appeal to Busters.

Lately Christian thinkers and writers have joined the Buster bandwagon, running, as is usually the case, several years behind the vanguard. Much of their work is helpful; we quote from it. The more useful material tends to be in the area of description—defining the

Buster generation and its tastes and values, the ground that we have already covered. When it comes to prescription, however, we find very little creative or comprehensive thought. Much of it runs something like this: Busters respond to MTV's rapidly changing images. Therefore we should use multimedia in our worship. Busters like alternative music. Therefore we should use new forms of music when trying to communicate with them.

No doubt these insights are slightly helpful, but they are also superficial. To try to understand and reach Busters solely on the level of taste and preference may be sharp marketing but it is shallow thinking and threadbare theology. If Christians are truly to reach Busters with the transforming message of the gospel, we will need a radical revisioning of the way the gospel is both presented and understood. Nothing less than a new understanding of the timeless message of the Bible will do for a generation that is radically unlike any that has come before.

Timeless Function, Ever Changing Form

Providentially the gospel is both timeless and constantly fresh, rooted in ancient tradition and liturgy while still as jarring and contemporary as this morning's *New York Times.* Further, we who would communicate the gospel take our cues from the Bible, which, more than a "user's manual for life," is actually a breathtaking articulation of the deepest truths of reality and the source of a comprehensive world- and lifeview. The Bible provides a sufficient and wholly relevant framework for understanding Busters and the issues we face in our times.

Busters, we have seen, are the inheritors of a fragmented and torn world and inevitably are fragmented and torn people. The values of this generation are often arbitrary and random, reflecting a culture in which there is no longer any consensus on what our shared values should be—or whether or not we should even have shared values at all! Clearly, a piecemeal and partial understanding of the Busters will only contribute to the problem. Whatever our strategies for reaching Busters with the Christian message, they must be derived from a comprehensive, carefully reasoned and articulated understanding of the real questions Busters are asking. We must also demonstrate a willingness to offer real answers. In a world that has seemingly gotten too big to tell stories about, only a magnificent and enthralling story deeply rooted in reality and suffused with hope will do.

Any prescription for reaching Busters will be rooted in the story of what God is doing fundamentally in history, where he is taking men and women in this torn and fragmented world, and what this tells us about how we should then live. This will require telling the Christian story with different emphases and categories than the traditional four-point recitations of a gospel tract.

The best starting point for this new understanding is the first chapter of Paul's letter to the church in Ephesus. Here in an ancient document is an exhilarating explanation of God's activity in history, which is nothing less than tailor-made for the world that Busters currently inhabit.

A New Old Paradigm: Ephesians 1

In our most excited moments, words can only barely begin to express our feelings. The apostle Paul knew this feeling well. Our English Bibles cannot capture the ecstasy with which Paul begins his letter. His words spill over each other in one long run-on sentence as Paul describes the love, sovereignty, and grace of the God who has chosen his people not because of any intrinsic merit on their part but only because he loves them extravagantly and beyond reason. It is through Christ that God's people have been blessed "in the heavenly realms" with indescribable gifts. It is through his death and resurrection that God has granted his people forgiveness of sins and relationship with him out of his stockpile of riches, "lavished on us with all wisdom and understanding" (Eph. 1:3–8). He seems to want to scream out, "This is awesome!"

Paul then begins to tell us of the "mystery" of God's will. He does not explain the mystery immediately but chooses to emphasize at what point the mystery will take place. Tantalizingly Paul tells us that the mystery will "be put into effect when the times will have reached their fulfillment" (Eph. 1:10). Those familiar with the Bible will recognize here an idea elsewhere developed as the "last days," "latter days," or, more popularly, the "end times."[1] It is clear that whatever the mystery, it will take place in the climactic days of the earth's existence, at a unique and momentous time in God's unfolding of his program for the world.

There is a lingering sense in popular evangelicalism that the "last days" refer to a time in the future, immediately preceding the return of Christ, when, quite literally, all hell will break loose. Many believers imagine that whenever the last days come, they will be much worse than these days and that it would be much better for Christians to be swept away safely to their heavenly reward.

A careful study of what the Bible has to say about the "last days," however, reveals a reality simultaneously less lurid and more sobering. In virtually every instance in which the "last days" or a related concept is discussed, the writer is referring to the time in which he is living, not some distant future. For the writers of the New Testament, it was quite clear that they themselves were living in the last days, the climactic period of history ushered in by the birth, death, and resurrection of Jesus Christ and continuing to his second coming. We will discuss the implications of living in the last days shortly. For now it is enough to say that to Paul, he was (and we are) living in the momentous time in which God was (and is) moving history to a shattering climax. There is a sense in which apocalyptic themes mesh with the nihilism of the Buster generation. However, the biblical perspective, rooted as it is in the sovereignty of a good God who firmly controls history, turns nihilism into hope.

What is it that will happen when the times have reached their ultimate fulfillment? God will have completed his sovereign plan "to bring all things in heaven and on earth together under one head, even Christ" (Eph. 1:10). It would be difficult to overemphasize the importance of this astounding verse, so pregnant with meaning. Indeed we will argue that here Paul is setting out for us a framework within which we can most effectively understand and minister to Baby Busters.

Christ the Household Manager

Paul speaks of God's "administration" of his purpose. Curiously this is a term resonant with financial significance. Further, the passage makes it clear that a large part of God's will was to reveal Christ as the administrative "steward" (oikonomos) of God's cosmic household. In the times in which Paul was writing, a steward was one who was charged with the oversight of his master's estate. He was to manage and invest his master's money, oversee the day-to-day operations of the estate, and insure that all of his master's affairs functioned smoothly. In short, he was empowered to act on behalf of his master, in his master's best interests. Christ, then, came as God's household manager, entrusted with everything that was his Father's, particularly his Father's world. When we present this perspective to Busters, we can be sure that there will be tension at this point. This world is messed up; Busters know this all too well. If Christ is the household manager, he must be doing a lousy job! At this point in the story, we must go back to the Garden to understand this fully.

The First Adam

Careful readers of the Bible will discern yet another level to Paul's use of the imagery of the household servant. For Jesus was not the first man entrusted with managing God's estate. The original *oikonomos* came long before Jesus and was, in fact, introduced in the opening pages of the Bible. He was Adam, who was created by God; placed in the first Garden; and given dominion over, responsibility for, and stewardship of God's world. In tones of wonder the first two chapters of Genesis describe God's creation of the world, his creation of Adam, and Adam's joyous mandate to act as God's steward in partnership with Eve, his wife.

The story, so full of beautiful and, in retrospect, heartbreaking promise, takes a dark and unexpected turn in chapter 3. God had imposed on Adam only one condition: "You are free to eat from any tree in the garden; but you must not eat from the tree of the knowledge of good and evil, for when you eat of it you will surely die" (Gen. 2:16–17).

Faced with the serpent's wiles and his own wife's disobedience, Adam made the fateful decision to eat from the forbidden tree. It was a decision freighted with unbelievable significance. For when Adam ate, he, in that one moment, declared his independence from God. His belief that God was not truly good and loving became evident, and he instantly abdicated his responsibility as God's steward. The consequences of his decision haunt us today. When Adam ate from the forbidden tree, the perfectly harmonious relationships between God and man, between man and man, and between man and his environment were instantly ruptured. To illustrate this, Adam was cast out of God's presence in the Garden, pitted against his wife, and forced to struggle against his environment even to have food to eat (Gen. 3:16–24).

Although Adam's choice was a personal one, the implications of that choice were universal. The Bible makes it clear that, in some mysterious way, Adam acted for all of us when he chose to declare his independence. He was in effect our representative, and we share in the consequences of the living and eternal death his choice brought on. For our relationships with each other are often tortured and painful; we are not strangers to abuse, betrayal, and disappointment. As never before in our history, we are conscious of the fact that our environment is not always friendly to us. Famine and natural disasters bring death, destruction, and heartache. For our part, we are guilty of a wanton disregard for the delicate balance of the environment and are just beginning to reap the bitter harvest of our environmental pollution and neglect. And, most of all, we know what it is like to be alienated from God, separated from him by our stubborn rebellion, not believing that he is truly good and has our best interests at heart. Though most are unlikely to describe their experience in these terms, this is precisely where Busters live.

The Second Adam

If the story had ended with Adam, it would have been a sad and hopeless story indeed. Separated from God, forced to live in a disjointed and fragmented universe, we would have known no hope for seeing our shattered relationships remade, our relationship with God restored, and our tenuous alliance with the created order renewed. By the goodness of God, however (and it is while reflecting on this that Paul is nearly out of his mind with joy), there came a second Adam to set right what the first Adam had so grievously put wrong. This second Adam, of course, was Jesus Christ. This is Paul's theme in Romans 5 when he compares Adam's "trespass" with Christ's "gift," a passage worth quoting at length:

> But the gift is not like the trespass. For if the many died by the trespass of the one man, how much more did God's grace and the gift that came by the grace of the one man, Jesus Christ, overflow to the many! . . . For if, by the trespass of the one man, death reigned through that one man, how much more will those who receive God's abundant provision of grace and of the gift of righteousness reign in life through the one man, Jesus Christ.
>
> Romans 5:15, 17

What Paul is saying is that Christ accomplished what Adam failed to do *and much more!* Adam had rebelled against God, doubting his goodness and failing in his responsibility as the manager of God's household. Christ, on the other hand, had perfectly obeyed God, lived a life that at every turn acknowledged the goodness of God, died an agonizing death to take care of the consequences of Adam's and our sin, and was raised to life to show that God ratified everything that he had done. Adam turned from God and, as a result, God's household, the world, was plunged into tortured disorder. Christ, the God-Man, embraced God's character and will with every fiber of his being and began his great task—putting God's household back together again. This was the task that he began through his death and resurrection and that continues today.

The Heavenly Ledger

We need to examine what Christ's administrative management of his Father's estate entails. Again Paul describes what God is doing this way: "to bring all things in heaven and on earth together under one head, even Christ" (Eph. 1:10). This bringing together (or "summing up" as some translations have it) is an accounting term used of totaling a column of numbers. In other contexts it is a rhetorical term, used to describe an orator's summation of his argument. Paul uses the idea when he speaks of the Ten Commandments relating to other people being summed up and integrated by the phrase "Love your neighbor as yourself" (Rom. 13:9). Colossians 1:22–23, a passage directly parallel to this Ephesians passage, explains the idea even further; there, Christ's headship or rule over all things brings about unity. What Paul has in mind, then, is nothing less than seeing "all things" ultimately brought together under the acknowledged rule and control of Jesus Christ, integrated under Christ's lordship. Even more to the point, this bringing together is a renewal of the conditions that existed in the Garden prior to Adam's rebellion against God. Christ is putting the pieces back together.

"All Things" Means Just That

Busters are quick to acknowledge that our world is torn apart. We are much less likely to agree, however, about what it is that needs putting back together. So what exactly is it that Christ is putting together? According to Paul, it is "all things (*ta panta*)," an inclusive term meaning everything in both earth and heaven—angels, men and women, rocks, trees, and animals.

Evangelicals have long had a penchant for neatly dividing things into two camps: "sacred" and "profane," or "Christian" and "secular." Hymns, prayers, evangelism, vacation Bible school, church buildings, and stained glass windows are "sacred" things; while money, nature, work, leisure, and sex are "secular," or so the often unconscious reasoning goes. Unfortunately this false dichotomy leads to a dichotomized life, which often seems suffocating and smug to those who do not follow Christ. Worse, the cultural captivity of many modern Christians has meant that far from being "in but not of the world" we are often "of but not in the world," having bought into cultural values while still maintaining a separate and artificial subculture. To borrow from Paul: Who will deliver us from this spiritual and cultural death?

Surprisingly our Eastern Orthodox brethren may be able to assist us. The Orthodox have long understood that the sacred/secular distinction is a false one. As a result their spirituality is a robust, holistic one, contemplating all of the created order, not just Sunday school and study Bibles. Christ is seen as Lord over all creation, including the environment and everything in it. It is a breathtaking, deeply satisfying spirituality, shot through with wonder and hope. While we certainly would not recommend that evangelicals adopt all of Orthodox theology (some of which is not particularly orthodox, incidentally), we do suggest that we can learn valuable lessons from it about how to view God's created order. As Abraham Kuyper, the distinctly non-Orthodox Reformed theologian and prime minister of the Netherlands said: "There is not one square inch in all of creation about which Jesus Christ does not say 'This is mine.'" Far from being a mandate for cultural or spiritual imperialism, this is a joyous recognition of the fact that all things are God's and that all things, when placed in their proper perspective, can bring honor and pleasure to God. Further, this understanding opens the way for us to present a holistic and comprehensive gospel, which has to do with real things—bread, wine, sex, trees, and rivers— and offers richly satisfying answers to the questions of those who live in a fragmented world.[2]

A New Community with a New Purpose

As we have emphasized, the world of the Baby Busters is a supremely fragmented one. How then can our treatment of Ephesians 1, the concept of the stewardship of Christ and the bringing together of all things in Christ, impact our ministry to Busters?

As followers of Jesus Christ, the church is called to image God in the world, to reflect his character and actions in our individual and corporate lives. We are to be "little Christs" in our world. It is not, of course, that we possess his supernatural abilities or his sinless perfection. We are most imperfect image-bearers. But as our character is gradually being transformed to be like Christ's, we will look more and more like him. As our wills are subsumed in God's will, our values will more and more resemble his. We will be more willing to give up our own personal ambitions, hopes, and dreams in favor of a heartfelt and passionate desire to be a part of what God is doing in human history. We will seek first his kingdom, becoming increasingly willing to give up our own personal empire-building. "Your kingdom come, your will be done" will be the fundamental expression of our heart's desire rather than a rote phrase.

Here is the crux of the matter: If we are right that what God is primarily about is bringing all things together in Christ; restoring shattered relationships; bringing unity and reconciliation between heaven and earth; and turning on its head the curse that separated man from God, his environment, and other men, then this is primarily what we will be about. Image-bearers are, by definition, to reflect the source of the image. As Paul was writing to the Ephesians, the issue in the forefront was reconciliation between Jews and non-Jews. That is just a small foretaste of the greater plan for cosmic reconciliation and unity, as all things are brought together under Christ's rule.

Today we live in a world torn as never before along lines of gender, race, socioeconomic standing, ethnicity, and values. If the gospel is being proclaimed authentically, it will be a reconciling rather than a polarizing force, bringing men and women together in Christ rather than dividing them. Christ himself will be the dividing point, nothing else. And the new community that Christ is calling together from every tribe, tongue, nation, and people group will demonstrate to a torn and tormented world that God is calling men and women to be reconciled to him and to become part of a new, reconciled community with an honest, holistic view of the gospel, thoroughly committed to joining God in his program of bringing all things together. Larry Crabb makes this point with great clarity:

God's course is clear: He has committed Himself to bringing "all things in heaven and earth together under one head, even Christ" (Eph. 1:10). If I want to walk with Him, I have no option but to join Him on that path. Agreeing to join Him requires that every other ambition in my heart become secondary to promoting Christ. Anything that contradicts this purpose must be abandoned.[3]

If we are going to speak to our generation so that we are heard, we must speak as men and women who understand that the world is fragmented and divided, who are honest in facing up to this fact, and who offer real answers and a real solution for this. We must present a gospel that speaks to all of life, not just the "spiritual part," and that is relevant to the concerns Busters feel about interpersonal relationships, the environment, racial and class prejudice, and ethnic diversity. In short, we must proclaim the gospel of Ephesians 1, the message of Paul, the good news about Jesus Christ, who is the one focal point for cosmic reintegration and the One worshiped by a new, reconciled community characterized by faith, hope, and love.

5

Living between the Already and the Not Yet

American Christians have long held a fascination for eschatology—the study of the end times, when God will bring the final curtain down on the history of this world. We love to construct elaborate schemes detailing how we think the end times will look, often in excruciating detail and full color. Ignoring Jesus' admonition that no one will know exactly when he will return (Matt. 24:42), we have often delighted in trying to pinpoint exactly that time.

Such eschatological excess has caused many to avoid the question of the end times altogether. This is unfortunate, not least because Jesus, in that same passage in which he says that no one will know the time of his return, urges diligence and vigilance. This theme runs throughout the Bible. In fact Bible scholars are increasingly coming to see that it is impossible to separate the message of the Bible from its eschatology; the Bible is supremely an eschatological book.

In the previous chapter we saw that the holistic vision of the New Testament is that God is working in history to sum up all things in Christ. This is God's eschatological thrust, and everything points to this consummation. We also saw that God is working through a new community composed of men and women from every nation and people group to carry out his purposes. We who are a part of this new community are to mimic God by focusing on putting things back together again and producing reconciliation in our world.

Welcome to the Kingdom

This summing up and reconciliation does not take place in a vacuum. Rather, it occurs in the context of what the Bible calls the "kingdom of God," a hugely important theme of the New Testament. To the writers of the New Testament, the kingdom of God was not a geographical sphere but rather the rule and reign of God in the lives of people. The kingdom "is to be understood as the reign of God dynamically active through human history through Jesus Christ, the purpose of which is the redemption of God's people . . . and the final establishment of the new heavens and the new earth . . . it means nothing less than the reign of God over his entire created universe."[1]

A Distant Hope Realized

To the writers of the Old Testament, the coming of the kingdom was a far-off event, a time when God would intervene in history to restore his people from exile, return glory to Israel, punish wrongdoing, and exalt those who obeyed and served God. Often this hope was summed up in the concept of "the day of the Lord," a day when God would come in crushing judgment against those who mocked him (Isa. 2:12, 17; Amos 5:18) and to save those who had remained faithful, creating a new heaven and a new earth (Isa. 65:17). The kingdom's coming would bring a new and permanent covenant between God and man, superseding the former covenant based on the Old Testament law, which Israel had broken time and again (Jer. 31:31–32).

Although the term "kingdom of God" is not found in the Old Testament, the thought is there—a hope for a day when God will make old things new and reestablish his relationship with his covenant people.

Jesus spoke about the kingdom of God more than almost any other topic. In doing so he made the extraordinary declaration that he himself was ushering in the kingdom; indeed, he was synonymous with the kingdom (Matt. 12:28; Luke 11:20).

In the wake of his ascension back to heaven and before his coming again, the kingdom is coming slowly and subversively, as more and more men and women acknowledge God's rule and reign in their lives. All this takes place in the context of the new community, the church, where the effects of the kingdom are seen most clearly. The church itself is not the kingdom, but it is the showcase for the kingdom.

The writers of the New Testament clearly understood that the great events hoped for in the Old Testament had found their fulfillment in Christ, who had ushered in the kingdom. There is an important modification of the Old Testament concept of the kingdom, however, that is of crucial importance for us as we look at how eschatology speaks to Baby Busters.

Already, but Not Yet

Simply put, the coming of the kingdom, which appeared as one event to the Old Testament prophets, is actually a long process marked on either side by two significant eschatological events—the first and second comings of Christ. Bible scholars recognize this as inaugurated eschatology—the kingdom of God and the "last days" have begun, but they have not yet reached their fulfillment.[2] The first coming of Christ and his death and resurrection began the final act of human history, which will culminate in his second coming to rule over all creation, the summing up of all things in him, the judgment of all men, and the creation of the new heaven and new earth. The kingdom of God is now present and is ever growing, but it grows subversively, often under attack and certainly not acknowledged by all.

The concept of inauguration is not altogether unfamiliar to us. When a new president of the United States takes the oath of office on a January morning, he is at that moment the president of the United States. He will never be "more president" than he is at that moment. Yet no one would say that his presidency is complete; that will not be for another four or eight years. His presidency is inaugurated—he is fully president—but his presidency is not yet all it will be.

Similarly historians agree that when Allied troops crashed onto the beaches of Normandy in 1945, the war in Europe was in effect finished. However, D-Day did not mark the end of the fighting. There were intense battles to be fought, thousands of troops to deploy, and much blood to be spilt before V-Day brought an end to the conflict.[3]

Here is the point: In terms of biblical eschatology, we are at this moment living in between D-Day and V-Day, in the midst of the inaugurated reign and rule of God. The outcome is certain—Christ's death and resurrection made sure of that—but the battle is not yet over. Not yet has every head bowed and every tongue confessed that Jesus is Lord; not yet has God's rule and reign been universally acknowledged; not yet are we all that we are going to be; not yet are we living in the new heaven and the new earth. We are caught between the *already*—the coming of Christ, our remaking as new creations, the beginning of the new community, the beginning of the slow process of summing up all things in Christ—and the *not yet*—the final triumph of good over evil, the defeat of pain and suffering, the return of Christ, the final summing up of all things in Christ, and the new heaven and new earth.

Those who love Christ rejoice greatly in the already, in the life we have in Christ, in the new community in which we live, in those exhilarating moments when another man or woman enters the kingdom. Yet our hearts are broken and incomplete because the not yet has not yet come. There is still injustice and pain and suffering and sin and tragedy and disease. There are still those who do not acknowledge God's rule and even actively oppose the kingdom. Even though we have experienced "the firstfruits of the Spirit," we now "groan inwardly," waiting for our ultimate and final adoption as sons and daughters of God (Rom. 8:23).

The fact that we live between the already and the not yet explains why talk of the "victorious Christian life" often rings shallow. Pain-free, prosperous living with all of our ducks in a row and lavish creature comforts to boot sounds wonderfully American but suspiciously nonbiblical. Those who have faced up honestly to the biblical text and to their own experience are much less likely to think of themselves as "saints who rarely sin," preferring instead to acknowledge that they are sinners made new creations only by God's grace.

For people who understand what it means to live between the already and the not yet, life is filled with both joy and sadness and is a long, slow pilgrimage of obedience and love for God and others, punctuated by times of deep sadness and moments of outrageous and holy joy. "Already–not yet" people do not relate to others in superficial ways nor do they give cheery Christian platitudes or easy answers and simplistic systems of discipleship. They are deeply rooted in God's grace and compassion, filled with joy, yet well acquainted with grief.

Kingdom Coming

The world we have described, this world in birth pains as depicted in Romans 8:22, is the world that our generation has inherited. In fact we can argue convincingly that the birth pains have never been as intense in our culture as they are at this moment.

Baby Busters are caught between the already and the not yet, but, as a generation of people, we lack the hope that the already brings. The need is for already–not yet people to move into the lives of Busters with both the passion and compassion of Christ, full of sadness for the condition of the not yet world and hope for what is possible now and to come.

This will mean that as we address Busters, we will not offer easy answers. We will not promise that the Bible holds a direct answer for every human dilemma or that becoming a follower of Christ will heal a broken family or clear up an uncertain future. We will acknowledge and share the pain of living in a broken and fragmented world, never minimizing the pain of broken people. The fact is that Christians, of all people, should never be surprised by pain and suffering; those experiences are so much a part of what the Bible says being human is all about.

On the other hand, we will dare to offer reckless hope in the midst of pain and suffering, simply because we *have* experienced the already of Christ and know what a difference that makes. Becoming a friend of God through following Christ means that healing, peace, and interpersonal reconciliation are possible. The Holy Spirit who invades the heart of every new believer will work to create permanent change by refining character and directing the heart's desire toward God and others.

One of the authors has been spending time with a Buster who is very close to choosing to follow Jesus. As he contemplated what it would look like to be a friend of God, his greatest excitement was at the prospect of moving into others' lives to bring the comfort and challenge and change that come with the gospel.

Let us remember that the opportunity we have to bring others to God is not only a rare privilege but also a remarkable thrill. We should view it with intense excitement. We must be bold in holding out the promise and hope of change to Busters who may hate both their relationships and their worlds.

We can also relate the already–not yet reality to the public issues most important to Busters. Until we grasp the implications of inaugurated eschatology, we are ineffective when faced with social crises. On the one hand, we may be so consumed with alleviating pain, suffering, and injustice that we lose sight of our theological framework and the fact that we live in times prior to the not yet, when there will be no more pain, suffering, or injustice.

On the other hand, we may despair at the desperate condition of the world and retreat into shells of comfort and disengagement ("After all, didn't Jesus say that we would always have the poor with us and that there would always be wars and rumors of wars?"). There is a middle ground between frantic political activity and sitting back and waiting for the end of the world. We can call it hopeful engagement with the world, with an eye toward the summing up of all things in Christ.

Substantial Healing

Hopeful engagement means that we move into the world with sober minds, well aware that we will not be able to fix every problem, end all suffering, or stop every injustice this side of the not yet. But we can hold out hope for what Francis Schaeffer called "substantial healing." Because God is a God concerned with putting broken things back together and bringing about reconciliation, and because we are to mimic God with our lives, we can expect that our hopeful engagement will have positive effects and, more importantly, will lead to God's glory in the sight of men and women. We can plunge into the AIDS crisis, work across racial lines to find solutions for the violence of the inner cities, and get involved in theologically responsible environmental action because God is pleased by this and because we can offer hope in these areas. Again Hoekema is on target:

> It is commonly thought by many Christians that the relationship between the present world and the new earth which is to come is one of absolute discontinuity. The new earth, so many think, will fall like a bomb into our midst. There will be no continuity whatever between this world and the next; all will be totally different. This understanding, however, does not do justice to the teaching of Scripture. There is continuity as well as disconti-

nuity . . . well expressed in words which were often used by medieval theologians, "Grace does not destroy nature but restores it" . . . this principle means that the new earth to which we look forward will not be totally different from the present one, but will be a renewal and glorification of the earth on which we now live.[4]

As we engage our worlds hopefully and give reasons why Busters should do the same, we should have the mindset of already–not yet people. We expect the consummation of all things and have our hearts tuned expectantly for the final curtain, but we engage the world as if we were going to be here forever.

We have talked much about how God's people are to mimic God as they live their lives both as individuals and as a corporate community. Outreach will confront the realities Busters face in their worlds without flinching. The gospel will not be presented as an abstract panacea but rather as good news that brings hope and has an impact on all of life. Christian Busters will develop a careful philosophy of public engagement and will throw themselves into important issues out of an eschatological framework, which has as its goal the glory of God.

In interpersonal relationships we can meet Busters as hopeful yet sad people. We will have deep empathy and compassion, tempered by a reckless hope that ultimately things will get better—if not now, then in God's future. In small groups, one-on-one meetings, evangelistic communication, and mentoring relationships, we will be already–not yet people, pressing hope into hopeless lives.

Hope for Now and Then

As we communicate the gospel to our generation, we are realistic people who have come to grips with the fact that we live this side of the not yet that God will bring. And we are joyful people who have tasted the already God has brought in Christ and know its promise. We are compassionate people who remember what it was like to live without Christ in this time of eschatological tension. But most of all we are hopeful people who dare to believe that God will one day complete the process that he began from the very beginning of time, the event for which ancient Israel waited with longing, the time that John heralded and Jesus proclaimed, the breaking into history that was the life, death, and resurrection of Christ, and the final climactic victory for which we await in this in-between time.

We are a generation that has been promised the moon by media communicators, politicos, and teachers preaching the gospel of self-esteem. The promises have proven empty. But we who love Christ are offering Busters something that is real and true. It is something that will find its full expression in the time of the not yet but that is already real in this time of waiting and expecting. "For in hope we have been saved," wrote Paul, "but hope that is seen is not hope; for why does one also hope for what he sees? But if we hope for what we do not see, with perseverance we wait eagerly for it" (Rom. 8:24–25 NASB). We have hope now as we live in between the already and the not yet.

6

Hope for the Hopeless

If the anguish, empowerment and ennui of "a denial" at the end of "Smells Like Teen Spirit" doesn't prove the anger that would lead a generation to commit suicide, then Kurt Cobain died in vain after all.

Letter to the editor of *Rolling Stone*

A Tale of Two Cities

Aberdeen is a long way from Seattle, at least by contrast. A once-bustling lumber town since fallen on hard times, Aberdeen is a gray ghost of its former self and going nowhere. Seattle, on the other hand, fairly teems with life. America's sweetheart city of the 80s, Seattle is gorgeous, filled with magnificent vistas, great coffee, and a diversity of cultural activity.

Seattle is also the spiritual home to the rock music movement of the early 90s—grunge rock. With its dense layering, raw lyrics of angst and alienation, and its turbulent undertones, grunge spawned a flannel-clad, boot-wearing subculture. The pioneers of grunge, however, were unquestionably the band Nirvana, fronted by the tortured, brilliant Kurt Cobain.

Cobain was a native of Aberdeen, an heir of its decline. Once a bright, artistic, and cheerful child, his parents' divorce when he was quite young triggered a downward spiral into rebellion, relational disengagement, and drug use. His one consolation during his dark teen years was music. His manic guitar playing, wry, angry lyrics, and raw, compelling voice were his signature early on.

In the late 80s, he formed Nirvana with a high school friend. They went through a succession of drummers and released an all-but-ignored first album. Sporting a new drummer and producer, they returned to the studio and recorded *Nevermind,* which was released in 1991.

No one could have foreseen the impact that one album would have. It exploded like a bombshell in the popular music world, selling millions of copies and transforming grunge from a regional oddity into a national obsession. "Nirvana," said one music critic, "turned the 80s into the 90s." The first track of the album, "Smells Like Teen Spirit," an electrifying ode of alienation, became the anthem of a generation. "Here we are now, entertain us," screamed Cobain in the song, "I feel stupid and contagious." *Newsweek* magazine wrote, "This was the sound of psychic damage, and an entire generation recognized it."[1] Cobain also captured the spirit of the seemingly apathetic Buster generation perfectly with the phrase, "Oh, well, whatever, nevermind," and he left his listeners breathless with the closing line sung over and over in defiance, "A denial!"

Overnight Cobain became the reigning, reluctant icon of his generation, an arbiter of right and wrong, cool and uncool. He became the moralist of a generation too, with his credo, "Hate, hate your enemies; Love, love your friends; Find, find your place; Speak, speak the truth." Never comfortable with the attention, always ill at ease with others, the most lasting image of Cobain is him hunched over an acoustic guitar, clad in trademark cardigan sweater, long dirty-blond hair hanging in his eyes, mumbling the lyrics to his song "Pennyroyal Tea." It was entrancing. It was also nearing an end.[2]

There was always a self-destructive side to Cobain. You could see it in his drug use, sense it in his lyrics, realize its presence in the painful stomach ailment that threatened to eat his insides out. It was, then, an unsurprising surprise when Cobain walked away from a drug treatment program, bought a shotgun, climbed into a little room above the attic in the Seattle house he shared with his wife and baby daughter, and blew his brains out. He left a rambling, angry, sad suicide note that explained little other than that he found little joy in music, his reason for being.

Crowds gathered near Cobain's home in Seattle to mourn. Fans wrote letters to *Rolling Stone* magazine. Two high school girls wrote that they heard the news during lunch. "When one friend of ours found out about Kurt," they wrote, "she went hysterical and went to her locker and grabbed a whole bunch of Advils and tried to get them in her mouth, but thankfully, they got wrestled from her hands. We let her have two for her headache."[3]

A reader of *Details* wrote: "Kurt Cobain and the music of Nirvana captured the feelings of myself and millions of others who, like Cobain, are trying to get a grip on our lives in a world where hopelessness, despair, and confusion are becoming the normal state of existence. When

Cobain said he survived his latest bout with drugs, depression, and other problems, I felt there was hope for him. . . . Most of all, I felt there was hope for those of us who identified with his music. Now that Cobain decided to give up, what fate awaits the millions who felt the way he did about the world?"[4] What fate, indeed.

Kurt Cobain escaped the hollowed-out industrial shell of Aberdeen, a town full of dead-end dreams and shattered hopes, and made it all the way to the bright lights of Seattle. It all seemed to be the perfect rags-to-riches success story; boy escapes dead-end life, makes it big, and heads toward a limitless future. He achieved fame and fortune and the status of spokesman for a generation. He loved a wife and fathered a daughter. Millions adored him. But he lived a life ultimately devoid of hope. And he killed himself in solitude in an empty room above his attic. Maybe the bright lights of Seattle simply serve to blind us to the reality that hopelessness is no respecter of success, money, popularity, or social status. Maybe Aberdeen isn't so far from Seattle after all.

Living without Hope, Then . . .

He was the embodiment of a hopeless generation, yet there have been hopeless men and women like Kurt Cobain since time immemorial. The apostle Paul knew a few and he wrote about them. In 1 Thessalonians 4:13, he compared Christians facing death with confidence with those who don't know Christ and thus must grieve without hope. In Ephesians 2:12, he has a devastating description of the state of those not in relationship with Christ: "having no hope and without God in the world" (NASB).

And Now

Perhaps unintentionally, the novelist Douglas Coupland picks up on this theme in his collection of stories *Life after God,* "You are the first generation raised without religion," trumpets the book's dust jacket, and the theme of the book is how to survive and cope in "a culture seemingly beyond God." The world Coupland describes is bleak and bare yet somehow not beyond hope.[5]

In one of the stories, the narrator is making a long solo car trip through the desert when he decides to tune in to a Christian radio station. His analysis of what he hears is just acute enough to make Christ-followers uncomfortable: These religious types take things too literally and miss the point sometimes. They project their needs and hurts onto Jesus in a way that alienates others who don't share their particular life experiences. "I did not deny that the existence of Jesus was real to these people—it was merely that I was cut off from their experience in a way that was never connectable. And yet I had to ask myself over and over what it was these radio people were seeing in the face of Jesus. They sounded like their lives had once been so messed up and lost as they spoke; at least they were no longer so lost anymore—like AA people. So I figured that was a good thing."[6]

This neatly sums up the Buster generation's plight of facing a seemingly hopeless world. Face reality, come to grips with the fact that life is neither fun nor fair, and deal with it. Past generations may have looked to the church or to historic Christianity for answers. Not this one. Christianity is not so much untrue as irrelevant, not a live option for a 90s person. And so those who live in a hopeless world and make up a generation without hope seem to have no interest in the message that is the only ultimate source of hope.

Trading Pearls for Pennies

According to the New Testament, the central realities of the Christian life are found in the triumvirate of faith, hope, and love. Although the gospel is radically countercultural, it is interesting to note that these three concepts are still valued in our postmodern times. It is a good thing, we are told by our godless culture, to have faith in something, even if it is "the god within." Love has never gone out of style and remains popular today; just ask Barney the purple dinosaur. And who would argue against hope? With nearly every new election, pundits write of a dramatic upsurge in hope sweeping the nation.

The only problem with this picture is that the Bible and the culture define faith, hope, and love in radically different ways. In the contemporary lexicon, faith can have as its object just about anything; love is often sloppy sentimentality shared when it is convenient; and hope is an ephemeral thing, ebbing and flowing with things as temporary as a political election. In contrast the Bible presents faith, hope, and love as blood and guts reality, strong beer and beef for anemic souls. Biblical faith is of epic proportions, evoking images of lions' dens and screaming, bloodthirsty Roman crowds. Love gets down on its hands and knees and washes dirty, sweaty, dusty, grimy feet. And hope clings to confidence in the midst of the most severe tests, continuing when all reason for hope seems to have vanished like a morning mist.

In the Bible, faith, hope, and love are not emotional conveniences designed to make a difficult life just a bit more palatable. Rather they are in-your-face real, effecting lasting life-change and softening hardened hearts. And most important, they are rooted in concrete historical realities: the demonstrated character of God in history; the life, death, and resurrection of Jesus Christ; and the reckless hope that one day God will turn tragedy into triumph and that good will win out over evil in spite of the long odds.

Faith and love, understood in the full-orbed biblical sense, will have an impact on Busters. But for our times, the theme of hope shows unique promise for speaking to the hopes, fears, and dreams of our generation. Hope is rooted in the past, real in the present, banking on the future. It is romantic, reckless, and countercultural. And it is just what our generation desperately needs.

A Good Track Record

The Bible is the book that contains the history of God's dealings with mankind in the past, present, and future. A constant theme through both Testaments is the faithfulness of God, often shown in stark relief to the faithlessness of men and women. Sprinkled throughout the pages of the Bible are the stories of men and women who dared to live recklessly and counterculturally, choosing to place their hope and faith in God, acting in obedience to him even when to do so seemed senseless. Noah put his hope in God's good intentions in the face of logic and ridicule. Sarah and Abraham hoped against hope that God would fulfill his promise to give them a child. Daniel chose a lions' den over political and vocational advance, not to mention personal safety. And many of the early followers of Jesus, witnesses of his death and resurrection, willingly gave their lives to advance the spread of his message.

Today we can turn to the Bible and read in story after story the record of God's covenant faithfulness to his people. The story of God's dealing with men and women in history is proof positive that his essential character is trustworthy. This means that we can, like Sarah, hope against hope. We can have firm confidence that the same God who came through for his people again and again will come through for us—indeed, more than "come through." The Bible is clear that God is sovereign, directing the course of events to bring about his ultimate intention, the culmination of the story where good triumphs over evil at last. "Whatever was written in earlier times," said Paul, "was written for our instruction, that through perseverance and the encouragement of the Scriptures we might have hope" (Rom. 15:4 NASB). A generation without hope needs to be told these stories for the first time; stories of passion and intrigue, suspense and romance, love and loss, fear and hope.

The Grand Demonstration

Everything in the Bible, in some way or another, ultimately points to Jesus Christ, the hero of the story. We get our first intimations of him in Genesis 3, where God promises to send one who will crush Satan's head. The unfolding of the story of the people of Israel, which comprises the remainder of the Old Testament, is the story of God working in and through a people to bring this one forth. The religious and sacrificial system of the Israelites foreshadowed the one who would finally set things right between God and man. As the Old Testament folds into four hundred years of silence, there is a heightened sense of anticipation that the promised one will soon come.

John the Baptizer bursts onto the scene as the New Testament opens. His self-proclaimed mission: to prepare the way for the one for whom the people have so long waited. This promised one, it is soon clear, is Jesus Christ, who moves boldly through his short ministry pronouncing the coming of the kingdom of God, working great miracles, making extraordinary claims about himself, and gathering a new community around him.

The men who recorded the events surrounding Jesus' life on earth make it clear that the culmination of his ministry, the culmination of the Israel-story, indeed, the culmination of the world's story, comes in the stunning events of the three days that saw Jesus' arrest, trial, execution, and resurrection. This is the climax of the story, the apogee of the great tale. It is truth greater than any fiction.

The events of these three days are, if we believe the narrative, the most important happenings in human history. In his death and resurrection, Christ took the hopeless case of mankind, estranged from God and one another, and turned tragedy into triumph. He died gruesomely; tormented physically, psychologically, and spiritually. And the most staggering fact is that he did it for us, on our behalf. "God made him who had no sin," wrote Paul, "to be sin on our behalf, so that we might become the righteousness of God in him" (2 Cor. 5:21 author's translation).

The fundamental reality of the human condition is that men and women are separated from God because of their sinfulness. This stark reality is darkened further by the fact that they are unable to do anything at all about this. Behind the sociological, psychological, and even theological explanations for the world the Busters have inherited lies the fact that the sinfulness of man has plunged the universe into disorder and disrepair. Our world is fragmented because we sin. Many Busters grew up in broken homes because people are sinful. The environment is threatened because people sin. There is drug abuse and inner-city violence because people sin. Any theology that does not come to grips with the sobering fact that sin is at the root of our problems is less than a Christian theology and must be rejected.

The most fundamental reality of the character of God is that he is a loving, holy being who, startlingly, pursues the same sinful men and women who have rejected his rule, killed his prophets, and executed his Son. God is one who "devises ways so that a banished person may not remain estranged from him" (2 Sam. 14:14). This is the most unlikely love story in all of history. It is too good to be true or, rather, too good *not* to be true.

This is the message that we have to tell lonely, rebellious, alienated, saddened, relationally shattered men and women: There is hope, even though things seem hopeless. But this hope is not found in yourself, in your ability to adapt and survive or to fix your own life with the help of good friends. It is a hope utterly outside of yourself and the people who have let you down and whom you have disappointed. It is a hope rooted in historical fact and a proven track record. It is a hope born of a breathtaking sacrifice. You are loved by Jesus Christ, who fully demonstrated his love in the language of nails and blood and pain and death. And he rose from the dead to show that God validated what he had done.

Because he died, you can be in relationship with God in spite of who you are and what you have done. Because he lives, you can also live, both now and in eternity. Because he came to shatter walls of hate and alienation, you can now pursue others and relate to them deeply. You can move into your world to knit it back together, addressing drugs and illiteracy and violence— only now you are operating out of God's resources, not your own. You can lose your life only to find it. You can forgive because you have been forgiven. You can love because he loved you first. Now you can experience the reality of the "God of hope fill[ing] you with all joy and peace in believing, that you may abound in hope by the power of the Holy Spirit" (Rom. 15:13 NASB).

A Reckless Hope

A young woman named Karen in a large city loves Jesus Christ and because of this, loves people with AIDS. One day a young man was hit by a car in the street outside of Karen's office. As he bled profusely from a punctured artery in his arm, police on the scene shrank back. You see, it was widely known in that community that the young man was a homosexual who had tested HIV-positive. Karen took in the scene from her office window and saw that the young man would soon bleed to death. She raced out into the street, broke through the ranks of onlookers and police, took the young man in her arms, and plunged her fingers into his wound to stop the flow of blood, all the while speaking soothing words of comfort.[7]

Rational? Prudent? Farsighted? None of the above. But the fact of the matter was that Karen had been gripped by something beyond herself, a love that had invaded the dark spaces of her heart and scattered light and hope. Karen had stood in full view of the death and resurrection of Jesus Christ, and her life had been changed. She had become a loving, reckless, passionate person, whose actions that day in the street were charged with hope. Hope that there was more to life than life, and hope that men and women whose hearts have been transformed by Jesus Christ can make an eternal difference in the lives of hopeless people. When your life is rooted in loving the God of hope, suddenly there are no hopeless situations, no hopeless generations. And that makes all the difference.

This was a hope that Kurt Cobain was never able to find. Faced with health problems, relational turmoil, addiction, and depression, he made the only logical choice, given his worldview. From the despair of Aberdeen to the illusory promise of Seattle, the hopelessness remained and led to the self-hatred of suicide.

Sadly Cobain never acknowledged that his tale of two cities could have had a final chapter. It is the story told near the end of the story, the tale of the Third City, the New Jerusalem—the city where hope will be satisfied and rewarded at long last, where the God of hope will be ever before the eyes of his people, where "He shall wipe away every tear from their eyes, and there shall no longer be any death; there shall no longer be any mourning, or crying, or pain; the first things have passed away" (Rev. 21:4 NASB).

We all live in a seemingly hopeless world, a world that is out of control, filled with violence and hatred and injustice. Yet those of us who know Jesus have a hope that transcends this temporary despair. God can be trusted to be good and to come through for us. We do have a hope that does not disappoint us.

PART
3

IMPLICATIONS

7

Telling the Old New Story

A Generation without a Story

Any self-respecting Buster will feel at least a twinge of resentment when he or she sees a car bearing the bumper slogan, "We're spending our children's inheritance." It's too close to the real truth. In Coupland's *Generation X,* Dag destroys such a car, a perfectly senseless (if perfectly understandable!) act. He offers this by way of explanation: ". . . the world has gotten too big—way beyond our capacity to tell stories about it, and so all we're stuck with are these blips and chunks and snippets on bumpers."[1]

The three friends who are the lead characters in the novel have moved to Arizona and spend their days in the desert telling one another stories. The stories are poignant, melodramatic, silly, and nostalgic. They borrow heavily from old TV shows and other popular cultural icons. It is painfully obvious that there is no unifying story that brings the three lives together.

When Coupland writes, "Either our lives become stories, or there's just no way to get through them," he is tacitly acknowledging that hope for finding a story worth telling and believing seems lost. The popularity of the talk-show highlight TV program *Talk Soup* proves that if we don't have our own stories, we will simply enjoy the bizarre stories of others. What else is there to do? Find refuge in virtual reality, live vicariously in the stories of others, or wistfully recall a less complicated childhood lived with Gilligan and the Skipper, the Beav, and Mr. Ed? Without a sense of being connected to a larger story, we are left only to pursue the philosophy of a tennis shoe commercial: "Be your own hero."

A World without a Story

In a groundbreaking article, Robert Jenson argues that our postmodern culture is one that has "lost its story." He notes that over the last several hundred years our culture has had a common heritage rooted in the biblical tradition. Although not everyone in the culture believed in the truth of the biblical narrative, and some in the culture were antagonistic toward it, there was still a widespread sense that the Bible contained the traditions that had informed and shaped the best of our corporate life. By and large, people knew the biblical story, and most saw the narrative as their story, at least in that it made sense of their world and their experiences with God and other people. In a very real sense, human life itself was a coherent story. A story with irony and twists and turns, to be sure, but a real story with real players moving to a real conclusion, shared in common by real people. We lived in a "narratable" world.

But as Jenson argues, this view of life is only possible in a culture that is shaped by the biblical tradition. That consensus has dissolved in the postmodern world. There is no longer an overarching story that explains everything. There is now a plethora of contradictory stories, none more valid than any other. In reality there is no longer a storyteller. And if there is no storyteller, writes Jenson, "then the universe can have no story line."[2]

Our generation has inherited this universe without a story line. And more than perhaps anyone else, we are acutely aware that our own lives have lost connectedness with a larger story.

Beyond the corporate story, we also need for our individual lives to have a story. And we need to share our stories with others. Our generation is yearning not only to tell our stories but also to feel that our stories are meaningful. Traditionally stories have knit families and communities together. They have helped to form a sense of deep community among friends and kin. The ritual of storytelling was an important and powerful anchor point in our life together, a way of actively participating in each others' lives.

Telling stories is as old as humankind, but we seem to sense a renewed understanding of just how important stories are in our lives. This reawakening has quietly stirred many thinkers and writers in recent years, including a number in the Christian tradition. In *Finding God,* Larry Crabb writes, "We in the Christian community need to tell our stories, risking shame and rebuke, because we want to find God."[3] He explains that our lives involve stories at many different levels; their plots are formed of relationships with others, with ourselves, and with our God.

Telling the Old Story in New Ways

If the Bible is anything it is a story. Full of pathos, intrigue, beauty, action, passion, and irony, the Bible as a work of literature stands alone. But unlike any other comparable work of literature, the Bible also claims to be True. We spell True with a capital *T* to illustrate the fact that far more than a mere claim to factual accuracy, the Bible claims to be the very word of God himself, containing the story of his character and his dealings in history. Moreover, the Bible is perhaps the only book in history that invites its readers to become personally involved and a part of its story. It claims to contain the story that is true for all people in all places and in all times.

Jesus recognized the importance of storytelling. Even a cursory reading of the New Testament Gospels reveals that he was a master storyteller. In his wonderful paraphrase of the New Testament, *The Message,* Eugene Peterson renders a portion of Mark 4 this way: "With many stories like these, he [Jesus] presented his message to them, fitting the stories to their experience and maturity. He was never without a story when he spoke."[4] Jesus knew that stories engage the listener, captivating both the intellect and the emotions. He knew that stories create links between people.

Sadly the Christian evangelical movement often seems to have lost sight of both the importance of storytelling and the sense of Scripture as story. Frequently the Bible is viewed as merely a sourcebook for doctrine, a guidebook of maxims for successful living, a manifesto for making public policy pronouncements, or a stick with which to beat others who are not like ourselves. And our evangelism often merely consists of offering a set of theological propositions that people must either accept or reject. While this is part of the truth, it is not the whole truth and is certainly not the part of the truth that will resonate most with Baby Busters.

Evangelist and author Leighton Ford makes the case that *narrative evangelism* is a form of telling the story that holds great promise for reaching Baby Busters in the postmodern world. Narrative evangelism is the act of living and telling this story to other people. For the narrative evangelist, the story is the message of God's activity in history, which leads to a new vision of who God is and how he views people. This new vision of promise and hope leads to the motivation for evangelism, which in turn leads to authentic character as people are changed by encountering the storyteller. "At some point in our journey through life," writes Ford, "our story collides with the Story of God—'the story with the large S.' God's Story calls our story into question. We must make a choice: either to reject the Story of God or to merge our story with His Story."[5]

It goes without saying that congruence between message and messenger is absolutely necessary for communicating with Busters, who are shrewdly sensitive to manipulation and quick to spot hypocrisy. For this reason alone, narrative evangelism deserves our careful attention. But this is not the only case for narrative evangelism. In addition we must acknowledge that it captures and illustrates a part of the nature of the Bible that we have often ignored.

And, not least, it works. Anyone who has been involved in proclamation evangelism, including the authors, would be quick to testify that an audience that grows bored and restless during the reciting of propositional truths will often give rapt attention to a well-crafted, engrossing story that communicates the same truth. One of the authors recently noted that a large part of his audience was suffering from glazed eyes as he spoke on the holiness of God. In midstream he told the story of a great Christian leader and his dramatic and highly personal struggles to come to terms with a holy God. Almost instantly the audience responded. You could have heard a pin drop. The reason? The story itself brought hearts to hear the message that it illustrated.

Another striking thing about stories is their versatility. They can communicate gently and quietly or loudly and with force. Jesus used both forms in his parables and stories. Often Jesus' teaching ministry was characterized by a bold directness. We read in John 3 that Nicodemus, a religious leader, came to Jesus late one night, when it was unlikely that he would be seen. Obviously ill at ease, Nicodemus began his conversation with Jesus by heaping up platitudes about his esteem for Jesus' reputation and teaching. Jesus cut him off instantly with a strong metaphor: "You must be born again!" Something about this direct, no-nonsense style appeals to our generation. A well-told story can communicate with the same urgency and directness. But only a certain kind of story will do. John Wesley said of Martin Luther's treatise "Bondage of the Will," "It has hands and feet." The same could be said of Jesus' storytelling. His stories are alive; they grab you. The same must be said of our storytelling if it is to captivate our generation.

By contrast many of Jesus' stories were so clever, so subtle, that some, including his disciples, scratched their heads in confusion, while others wandered off, seemingly unaware that they had missed a truth about the kingdom of God. The result was profound. It allowed those who had the desire to know God and understand spiritual truths to ponder and reflect more deeply. Consequently those with patience and diligence left with a rich understanding of their heavenly Father, while the self-serving opportunists left with nothing.

In reaching this generation, we take on the challenge to discern when to tell stories that hit hard and when to tell stories that speak quietly. Both kinds of stories are appropriate at different times and with different audiences.

Stories Good and Bad

A point of caution is in order here. Stories and parables must be told with skill if they are to be effective in communicating the gospel. The mere fact that a story is a Christian story does not make it a *good* story. There are whole bookshelves full of bad Christian stories that are full of spiritual truth but woefully inadequate as art. A good story will reflect and reveal rather than preach and propagandize. It is more a surprise than a lecture. A good story is more likely to make us love truth and beauty than it is to spur us to write a letter to the editor or call our representative in Congress.

This is why the stories of C. S. Lewis and of J. R. R. Tolkien are great stories and those of some more recent Christian authors are not. Lewis and Tolkien never set out to tell a *Christian* story. Their aim was to write a *good* story. They succeeded—gloriously. Because the men themselves were deeply committed to their faith, the Christian story is the glorious backdrop for both the Narnia and Middleearth tales. Christian truth is subtly present on every page, but the truth itself has such impact because its presentation is not calculated but is inevitable and authentic. On the other hand, some other authors set out with an agenda. They set out to communicate truth, and the story is merely a vehicle. No doubt they often do a fine job, but they are skilled as propagandists and not as storytellers.

To reach our generation we must dare to tell good stories for the sake of the stories, refusing to compromise on beauty or tension or any of the elements that make a story a real story. If we have a good grasp of Christian truth and if we are loving God and people, our stories, like Lewis's and Tolkien's will warm cold hearts, thaw frozen minds, and change lives.

There are dangers here of course. We can never forget that the gospel really is propositional truth that must be either accepted or rejected. However, the way in which that propositional truth is communicated can make all the difference between an eager response and indifference. Preachers who have been trained to deliver dry theological lectures thinly disguised as sermons must learn to communicate the same truth in story form to reach this generation. We will find ourselves using the medium of drama—which is uniquely adapted to storytelling—with increasing frequency. The paradigm for how we equip laypeople in evangelism must move from learning and reciting four-part outlines of gospel truth to cultivating a sensitivity to listen, see the big picture of the gospel and the modern world, tell the good news as a good story, and model the story with our own lives. In our communication—written and oral—we will learn to tell stories, to spin ancient truths in the form of modern parables that scatter light and cause flashes of insight.

Narrative evangelism and creative storytelling may well offer the best hope for pressing the story into the lives of Baby Busters. To fully utilize the potential of story will require a courageous revisioning on the part of the church of both theology and methodology. The extent to which the church is willing to adapt its methods while holding to timeless truth may well be the determining factor in the extent of its impact on the Buster generation.

Reaching the Generation with Stories

Stories play an important role for our generation in many different ways. As we have seen, the most obvious implication concerns how we communicate the gospel. We must rediscover the sense that the message of salvation is a story of a bold and marvelously creative rescue mission. We must learn to breathe life into old truths that have been beaten nearly to death by the culture. The parables of Jesus are our ultimate model. But we can find help in other places as well. The parables of the Danish Christian philosopher Søren Kierkegaard have arresting impact. We can read Lewis and Tolkien, George MacDonald, and Charles Williams. There is perhaps no better modern-day storyteller to learn from than Garrison Keillor! Many contemporary Christian writers, such as Brennan Manning, Philip Yancey, Walter Wangerin, and Calvin Miller also show how the truths of God's grace can be gently or boldly couched in the form of a story.

Preachers are often adept at using anecdotes to make their points, but telling good stories goes far beyond sermon illustrations. The best stories are our own. We can tell the stories of our struggles and joys as we live in complex relationship with God and those around us. We can tell our story of how we were rescued and how we fell in love with the Rescuer.

To tell our stories well, we must first believe that we are truly living rich dramas. Larry Crabb writes, "Each of our lives is a dramatic story of how a relational, passionate, thoughtful, purposeful, and depraved person handles the experiences of life."[6] We have much to tell in our stories and many opportunities to live heroically but, thankfully, we *can't* be our own heroes. Jesus is the hero.

8

Operating Values for the Generation

Let's get down to business by using a business metaphor. What can the church do to reach Busters with the transforming message of Jesus Christ? What form will effective ministry to Busters take right now? What themes should be emphasized?

First, a disclaimer is needed: Church and parachurch leaders who hope to find a four-step plan for effective evangelism to Baby Busters will be disappointed. We will not offer a model curriculum, stock sermon illustrations, church program portfolio, or prototype budget line items. This is a generation that has been marketed to death and is all too aware when it is being manipulated. Practitioners of "Xerox Evangelism"—to use Donald Posterski's phrase—need not apply to reach Baby Busters.

You have probably noticed by now that we like overarching themes and paradigms. We believe that understanding the big picture is absolutely necessary for effective ministry to anyone in the postmodern world. What we will offer, then, is a set of themes and parameters within which we believe the church can minister effectively to Busters. To do this we will borrow a concept from the world of business and commerce. In our next chapter we will suggest a few practical applications of the paradigms.

Operating Values That Boost the Bottom Line

This is the age of multinational corporations. They compete in a world brought together in stunning fashion by fax and modem and other advances in telecommunications. Geographical boundaries matter less than ever before as companies find that their enterprises must be comprehensive and far-flung. A CEO may be stationed in New York, while a vice president lives in Tokyo, a division manager in Sydney, an area director in Addis Ababa, and an administrative assistant in Duluth. Multinational corporations face the daunting task of giving some kind of coherence to their operations and of finding some kind of shared ethos and mission that can be held in common across millions of miles, several continents, and a dizzying variety of ethnic and cultural backgrounds.

Astute managers in the age of the multinational corporation know that they must establish, communicate, and instill ownership in a set of *operating values*. These are beliefs, tenets, and aspects of corporate mission that are known, shared, and acted upon by every member of an organization, from the highest executive to the most junior maintenance worker. These operating values transcend cultural boundaries and customs, serving as the point of convergence for a constellation of different life experiences, socioeconomic backgrounds, work settings, and ethnic heritages. Effective operating values provide unity in the midst of diversity, without minimizing the richness of the diversity.

Followers of Jesus Christ are part of the largest multinational corporation in the history of the world—the church of Jesus Christ! Drawn from every race, people group, country of origin, and economic subgroup, followers of Christ are united in their commitment to the shared operating values of faith, hope, and love. It is this mutual commitment to the essentials of the faith that can unite African American Pentecostals in Mississippi, staid Anglican worshipers in London, Wesleyan perfectionists in West Virginia, Southern Baptists in Texas, members of the Kale Heywet church in Ethiopia, and buttoned-up, starch-collared Presbyterians in North Carolina. Although it is often taken for granted, this built-in unity in diversity that is part of the Christian experience is one of our richest resources in an increasingly complex world.

The concept of operating values, which provides a framework for understanding Christian unity, also offers suggestions for effective ministry in the postmodern world. If we are right in our contention that Busters offer different challenges for contextualizing the gospel than we've ever faced before, and if we're also right that any approach to reaching the generation must take into account its individuality and diversity, then what we need are a set of operating values that will shape and inform our ministry to our generation. These will not be rigid categories but rather will sound themes that are crucial to Busters and to which the gospel speaks with urgency, relevance, and force. We must recognize at every moment that effective ministry to any cohort must allow an enormous amount of latitude for understanding their site- and situation-specific needs and concerns. Therefore, what we offer here is not so much a blueprint as a way of thinking. The three operating values for ministry to our generation are *creation, covenant,* and *community.*

In the Beginning

Any telling of the Christian story must begin with the beginning of the beginning—God's creation of the universe ex nihilo, "out of nothing." From nothing the Creator shaped all that is and pronounced it good. It was good because he made it, because it shared in something of his essence, in the same way that a sculpture captures something of the sculptor. God was and is evident in his creation, as Paul makes clear in Romans 1.

The crowning glory of the creation was mankind. Out of all the stunning creation, mankind alone was said to be created in God's image, bearing an unmistakable imprint of the Creator and thus alone able to relate to him personally. As we have seen, all of this promise was shattered in the moment when man declared his independence from God, revealing his fundamental belief that God was really not good after all. The very real freedom and knowledge that came from his rebellion came at a devastating price. Adam was separated from God. All of us who are his children are separated from God, excluded by birth from his special love and light. The earth has shared in this exclusion, often turning against itself and the people who live in it. Since Adam, it has been evident to all that something is rotten in creation, that something has gone sadly amiss, has been broken and desperately needs to be put back together.

Enter Christ, the cosmic Repairman. His life and death began the process of knitting back together the fabric of creation that had been ripped apart. Now we can taste the firstfruits of the ultimate and final reconciliation and summing up of all things in Christ. Relationships can be sewn back together, peace with God and others can be found, and we can work with God in mending and loving his created order.

This is, in essence, God's story. This is what he has done and is doing in space and time. He is bringing together a people for himself, re-creating individuals and whole communities in his image, preparing them for the day when all things will be re-created. Between the already and the not yet, we can mimic God joyfully as we once again exercise the rights and responsibilities of stewardship abdicated by Adam.

Creation and Evangelism

The concept of creation is vital for evangelism because it touches on so much of what it means to be human. It is particularly vital for evangelism with Baby Busters because it speaks to our generational situation with poignancy and passion.

We have inherited a world in which men and women have abdicated their stewardship like never before. This century has been perhaps the most violent and bloody in history; we have literally ripped each other apart. As industrialization and technocratization have achieved the status of religious values, we have raped and shattered our environment, and we are just now starting to realize the consequences of that.

On this large scale and on the smaller scale of relationships, we are desperately in need of re-creation, of restoration to the state of innocence and freshness Busters are unable to articulate but nevertheless sense was there millions of years ago. This is precisely what the Christian story says has happened in Christ. This is the Good News—we can be re-created and made new. If we will exchange our old life for the life of Christ, God will give us a fresh start.

Tasting Re-Creation

Christians have recoiled at the thought of embracing environmental issues for fear of becoming associated with the New Age and pantheistic philosophies often found among environmentalists. This should not be the case. Christians should embrace valid environmental concerns out of respect for the Creator. We should re-frame these concerns by directing our thinking past the creation itself and to the Creator and his capacity for re-creation. William Badke writes, "Evangelicals have missed the point that the earth is the Lord's and the things that happen to it mirror the heart condition of the people who inhabit it."[1]

The implications of a renewed understanding of creation and re-creation are wide and varied. Re-creation validates the concerns Busters feel for protecting and preserving the environment. Their energies in this direction can be affirmed and channeled into service to God. "Your desire to care for the environment is right and commendable," we can say. "We Christians have been slow to do the very things that you are doing, and we were wrong. However, you have to understand that the Christian story provides the only real understanding of the environment that can make sense out of what you are doing. The creation is God's. It does not have a personality of its own. Protecting the environment is a means to an end—loving and serving God, getting caught up in his story—rather than an end in itself. Commit your life to God's story, and you will find your energies for protecting creation redoubled."

On a very practical level, we can model creation stewardship. Churches can use recycled paper for their letterhead and do away with Styrofoam cups for coffee hour. We can set up recycling containers in our churches, ministry centers, and collegiate fellowship meeting places. Get members involved with a community-based environmental action group. Students especially can plug into environmental advocacy groups. This is a great way to build relationships with Busters while honoring God. Remember this is a generation that wants to see action at the individual and grassroots level.

The leadership of the church can also model a healthy view of biblical environmentalism. Pastors can preach and teach a biblical view of environmental stewardship. A church or consortium can host a community forum on "The Christian Faith and the Environment" that can serve as both equipping for believers and an outreach for nonbelievers with environmental concern. We should do these kinds of things not only because they will gain us credibility with our generation but because they are right and give honor to God.

Keeping Promises

Whatever else they may disagree about, biblical scholars are in accord that the concept of *covenant* is vitally important to understanding what is going on in the biblical story. In the ancient Near East, the world of the Old Testament, covenants and covenant-like agreements and treaties largely shaped everyday life. A solemn and binding agreement between two parties that required action on each side, a covenant was seen as the extension of the personality and integrity of the covenant makers.

When God chose to communicate his character and will to mankind, he chose the form of covenant. In many ways the Bible is simply the recording of the successive covenants made between God and man as history unfolded.

A key biblical covenant is the Abrahamic covenant, in which God promises that he will be uniquely related to the people of Israel. In return the people are to give their sole allegiance to God, worshiping, serving, and obeying him alone (Gen. 15ff.). If they keep their end of the bargain, they will receive military and economic success, peace, prosperity, and the inheritance of the beautiful and bountiful promised land.

As even the beginning student of the Old Testament knows, the people of Israel did not keep the covenant. Their history is a cycle of obedience and disobedience, covenant faithfulness and covenant unfaithfulness that serves as a stark contrast to their solemn vows. The cycle culminated in the climactic period of 760–460 B.C. During this three-hundred-year band of history, God sent the writing prophets to indict the people for their unfaithfulness, warn them of the judgment that was rapidly approaching, and plead with them to repent and turn back to God.

Somewhere in the midst of that period, the message began to change from one of hope to one of impending judgment. And in those terrible days, the people were split into two competing kingdoms, thrown into civil war, weakened economically, and finally conquered by foreign powers and scattered to the four winds. The people had finally and irrevocably broken the covenant, and God's judgment had fallen. The nation was no more, the voice of God through the prophets was silenced, and all hope seemed to have been lost.

But despair was forced to reckon with a covenant-keeping God, who would absolutely not go back on a promise he had made. The Old Covenant had been shattered but a New Covenant was coming. From the dust of the disobedience of the Israelites, God brought John the Baptizer, a figure remarkably like the Old Testament prophets. He sounded the same message of repentance and worship of God, with the same emphasis on a coming future hope. But in John that hope took a specific shape, embodied in Jesus of Nazareth.

John was preparing the way for Jesus the Christ, who would serve as the covenant-keeper for a group of people he would call to himself. Christ lived a perfect life, perfectly keeping the covenant requirements that the nation of Israel had so badly failed to keep. And in his death, he paid the death penalty for the covenant unfaithfulness of the people, wiping the slate clean and making it possible for men and women to come before God without the taint of covenant-breaking. His blood, which poured from his body during his gruesome death on a Roman cross, served as the covenant-ratifying element of a new blood covenant (Matt. 26:28). Unlike the previous covenant, which had been broken by the people, this one could never be shattered.

The essence of the gospel is that men and women can now be personally related to God by joining and accepting the New Covenant that God has made. This New Covenant is superior in every way to the Old (Heb. 8–10). It is unbreakable and irrevocable. It is for all time. It is not dependent on the efforts of men and women; Christ has perfectly kept the covenant, and his perfect covenant obedience is available to all who place their trust in him alone. It is inclusive; no longer limited to one religious-ethnic people, the New Covenant is open to all people everywhere (Gal. 3:26–29). This New Covenant is the fundamental reality that is to govern and shape the lives of followers of Jesus Christ.

Living the Covenant

The concept of covenant is not only thoroughly and unmistakably biblical, but it is uniquely suited to communicate the gospel to Baby Busters. Perhaps the most common experience for the generation is having promises and vows broken and disregarded. Our parents' marriage vows have been broken like no generations' in history. Our political leaders have lied to us time and again. For many of us, Watergate was our earliest political memory, we cut our teeth as high school and college students on the Iran-Contra scandal, and as post-grads we have watched Whitewater-gate unfold. Religious leaders have fallen by the dozen; our generation watched in disbelief as Jessica Hahn told her sordid tale of Jim Bakker's sexual antics and as lusty Jimmy Swaggart cried on cue, only later to refuse his church's discipline and any sort of accountability for his actions.

Though scarred by all these broken promises, we have already shown ourselves to be a generation apt to continue in the sins of our fathers. The Busters' lack of ability to form committed and whole relationships, our fear of commitment to anything outside of ourselves ("Best of all, no commitment!" proclaim CD and tape clubs that once required a minimum purchase of eight recordings over three years to join), and our willingness to skip from job to job and company to company ("No loyalty," pronounce Boomer bosses) are perhaps best understood as a fear of having any more promises broken. If you don't commit, you can't get hurt. If you ask for nothing real and offer nothing of substance, at least you're protected.

Beneath the cynical facade and the no-commitment rhetoric is a desperate hunger for authenticity and relationships that last beyond mutual gratification and convenience. It is at this point that Busters' hearts are wounded and tender. Will we care about them enough to love them with a sacrificial, selfless love?

Will we preach and practice covenant faithfulness, acting with costly integrity in our jobs, relationships, marriages, and responsibilities? Will Boomer believers with a heart for Busters reach out and form mentoring relationships based on trust, encouragement, and fidelity? Will churches spend their money wisely and carefully, avoiding debt as much as possible? To reach this generation, we must answer, "Yes, we will."

Homesick for the Home We Never Had

I'm homesick for a home I never had.

Soul Asylum

The band Soul Asylum nearly perfectly captures the ambiguity Busters feel about our world and our place in that world. This is a generation with a gnawing sense that something is not right, that there is more to relationship than we are experiencing. But for reasons that we have seen, most have no frame of reference with which to understand the conflicting longings we feel. We are homesick, but we have known no home to long for. In essence we are a group of individuals who are disconnected from any sense of community and belonging.

Busters pay lip service to the importance of community. Our demographic's TV shows and advertisements reflect this clearly. Buster-targeted shows such as *Beverly Hills 90210* and *Melrose Place* feature groups of Busters moving through life together in community. An ad for cotton reads: "There is no Generation X. There are no 'Baby Busters.' There is just you and your friends and the 40 million or so men and women of your generation who share common experiences, concerns, hopes, and values." Observe the Buster culture, and it would be easy to conclude that its driving force is relationships and community.

But then why is it so clear that many Busters have no idea how to relate in healthy ways, that we are desperately starved for relationship and community? In large part it is because there is very little substance behind the rhetoric of community. The Busters are in many ways a microcosm of the larger culture, which for all the talk of "community"—the African American community, the arts community, the gay community, the Christian community—is increasingly fragmented and splintered. It is safe to say that many Busters had no chance to develop into people able to relate to others richly. Our families are too broken, our schools too violent, our models too confused.

Building a New Community

Along with the concept of story, the felt need of community may be the most promising point of entry for the gospel in our generation. Busters have a self-confessed need for community and relationship and idealize what it would be like to live in community. When we are honest, however, we acknowledge that we are not experiencing community and would probably not know what to do if we were ever to find ourselves in community.

The church can offer community to Busters desperate for relationship. Inherent in the idea of a covenant community is the fact that men and women are not called to follow Christ alone but are called *together* to love and serve

God and each other. The community of faith is to be made up of men and women who have encountered God's stunning grace in their own lives and are now committed to passing this grace and forgiveness on to others. The "one another" phrases of the New Testament, worthy of careful study, describe what life is to be like in the new community. Dietrich Bonhoeffer's often quoted description of Jesus as a "man for others" is an apt description of the follower of Christ. We are to give up our selfish ambitions, petty conceits, desires for comfort, security, and privacy, and involve ourselves deeply in the lives of others.

Our life together is to be characterized by selflessness, service, compassion, prayer, worship, and generosity. The injunction to "encourage one another" does not imply a slap on the back and a saccharine sentiment but rather a gutsy willingness to draw alongside of another, share her burdens and pains, and give of myself for her well-being. In our families and in the wider context of the church family, we are to model the perfect relationship and fellowship that exists between Father, Son, and Holy Spirit.

There are signs, such as the explosion of the small group movement, that the Christian evangelical movement is recapturing the importance of community. But we are now at a critical juncture. Will our explorations into living in community simply follow the shallow rhetoric and unfulfilled promises of the therapeutic culture? Or will we experience ourselves in community and model to the world the redemptive, forgiving, freeing love of Christ? A generation waits to see.

A Story Not Yet Finished

When the story of this storyless generation is written, will it be a joyous or a despairing tale? As things stand now, the prospects do not appear encouraging. Home-sick for a home we never had, without hope, and without God in the world, our generation appears headed for mindless mediocrity and tedious triviality broken only by occasional flare-ups of rage and alienation like the South Central Los Angeles riots.

Followers of Jesus, however, know that irony and sur-prise endings are Christ's specialty. God is uniquely able to turn tragedy into triumph; he demonstrated this con-clusively when he raised Christ from the dead. The story is not yet finished. There are twists and turns yet to come. The key player is the risen Christ himself, but others have parts to play as well. The supporting cast is com-posed of Christ's followers, a decidedly motley band of sinner-saints who have been empowered to turn the world upside down. A corporate life built around the operating values of creation, covenant, and community lived out by a group committed to renewal, promise keeping, and mutual love and commitment is a thrilling dream. It is a dream within the reach of those of our gen-eration who follow Christ.

9

Putting It in Place

Living in the Real World

The book market for church leaders is glutted with publications on how to reach Baby Boomers. After all, Boomers are now at the apex of their power and influence and are in effect the arbiters of societal taste and trend. To reach Baby Boomers is to reach many suburban communities.

Leaders looking for tools to reach Busters, on the other hand, have far fewer models to choose from. In part this is inevitable. Busters are by definition difficult to categorize; we value and practice diversity, and we resist being pigeonholed. And, in part, the market demands Boomer-focus.

From the beginning, we determined to resist a primarily methodological orientation for this book. For one

124

thing, we are convinced that a major weakness of the Christian evangelical movement is that it honors pragmatism over reflection. For another, others have written or are writing books and articles on how to program a church or parachurch ministry to reach Busters. Our goal has been primarily a theological and sociological one.

However, the end of reflection must always be action. We are both engaged in trying to reach Busters with the gospel. And we are committed to helping everyone we can do a more effective job in contextualizing the gospel for our generation and discipling Busters. We need help ourselves!

To that end we will take a brief look at some places where effective Buster ministry is already happening. It goes without saying that every ministry must be uniquely adapted to its own context; with Busters, especially, cookie-cutter ministry models will fail miserably. As we have surveyed effective ministries, we have noticed that they have many common themes. Most of them have created a true sense of community for their members. Most of them are organized around making each individual feel important and valued. Most of them know how to honor and use the culture. And most of them know how to accommodate change effectively.

Community

Much of this book, particularly the previous chapter, has been dedicated to arguing that the value of community, as much as any, captures the hearts and minds of Busters and that community is at the very heart of the gospel. We can boil Christ's mission down to this essential core: creating a new community of men and women from every conceivable ethnic, racial, economic, educa-

tional, and relational background, united by one thing—
a relationship with Jesus Christ as forgiver and leader.
Bill Mahedy is blunt: "Restoration of community is the
primary need of Generation X."[1]

The gospel demands radical community. And churches
that reach Busters provide a context for true relational
interconnectedness and interdependence. One college
student, Sheri, tells of her battle with leukemia. When
she lost her hair during chemotherapy, two of the male
students in her small group shaved their own heads and
posed for pictures with Sheri. "When the guys had bald
heads, too, I felt loved and accepted," Sheri said. "I didn't
have to be ashamed."[2] Real community involves identi-
fication with one another in love, the willingness to "bear
one another's burdens," even when the bearing is costly.

Janet Bernardi tells a fascinating story of her college
group's becoming a community. These friends began
to cook together to find "a community of people we
could trust." This "spirituality of dinner together" reflects the emphasis in the biblical culture of the ancient Near East on the sacredness of eating with one
another. "What we did," writes Bernardi of her college
experience, "was create a family, a community—something larger than ourselves, but not so large that our
individual actions did not have an effect. We sought
healing of our broken spirits in the community of others, and we found it."[3]

The value of community comes through loud and clear
in ministries that emphasize racial reconciliation, eating together, and sharing life. All communities can participate in community service projects together. Some
churches will want to encourage intentional geographic
community—actually living together. For some Busters
traumatized by abuse, this may be the only hope of learning to relate to others in healthy, nonmanipulative ways.

Of course each community will look and act differently. But regardless of where the community is located or what sort of people make up its constituency, there must be a baseline to real biblical community.

> The Church is the community gathered by God, and so it must offer examples of real community. The leaven among Generation X are those young adults who are forming communities among themselves and with God. For indeed there is a path out of loneliness and into transcendent hope. It lies in community, and ultimately in community with God.[4]

People

Jesus had a thing for people. To read the Gospels is to be gripped with the conviction that nothing mattered to Jesus more than individuals—their hopes, dreams, failings, sicknesses, sadness, and celebrations.

Dieter Zander founded New Song Church in California, almost the prototypical Buster-targeted church. More recently he has been hired as a teaching pastor by Willow Creek Community Church near Chicago (certainly the prototypical Boomer-targeted church!). Among his tasks at Willow Creek is to develop and launch a Buster ministry, known as Axis. Zander places a heavy emphasis on the importance of individuals. He uses the illustration of a meal to contrast Boomers and Busters. Boomers, he says, are likely to prefer an elegant seven course meal, beautifully prepared and presented, sauces and spices just right. Busters, on the other hand, are more likely to prefer a potluck, where each individual brings his or her own dish. It is messier this way—perhaps we will end up with all bread or all dessert, and I may not like the dish you bring. But the important thing is that *you* brought it and that I value you for your contribution.[5]

This concern for the individual overrides the concern for broad goals and plans. People are always paramount. However, there is an important nuance here that sets this value apart from the rampant individualism of American Boomer culture. The difference is that the individual is always viewed in the context of his or her community. Relationships come first.

People interested in becoming involved in leadership in the genX ministry at Forest Hill Church in Charlotte, North Carolina, are welcomed warmly and enthusiastically. However, no one, regardless of his gifts, skills, or talents, is given leadership right away. Everyone is welcomed the same way: "We're delighted to have you. We invite you to join the community. The task is simple: Hang out and invest your life here, and involve yourself with the community." Those who would lead must first be servants in the community. This servanthood is modeled by an overriding concern for individual others. This is what Kevin Ford has aptly called an "embodied apologetic" for the gospel.

Culture

We each live and move and have our being in the context of our culture, that set of assumptions and attitudes that inform the values, preferences, and beliefs for our lives and the lives of those around us. What we are most interested in here is one manifestation of culture—how truth and values are communicated in culture, the cultural forms by which people receive, understand, and appropriate truth. It should go without saying that we must communicate the same truth differently in different cultures; we would explain the Christian story very differently to a child in a Kurdish refugee camp than we would to an American prep school student.

To effectively communicate the gospel to Busters requires an intimate familiarity with Buster culture, which is quite different from the culture of previous generations. What is true of western culture in general is doubly true for those who would communicate to our generation. "Since western society is now a competitive arena for many religions, movements, and ideologies, and since the public's expectations of all communicators have been raised in the media age, the only Christians who will be taken seriously will be informed communicators."[6]

Since a large portion of this book has been dedicated to explaining Buster culture, we will not retrace our steps here. It is enough to say that churches and other ministries that want to reach Busters will take great pains to insure that their message is packaged and delivered in ways that are meaningful to the Buster culture. This will mean that the message will be highly visual and experiential. It will be ironic and irreverent; New Song Church in California used David Letterman as one influence for its Sunday morning outreaches. It will be relational; in its effort to make sure that "no one leaves without relating to someone," South Coast Community Church in Irvine, California, sets up round tables rather than seats, appoints table hosts, and draws everyone into conversation.[7]

Emmanuel Baptist Church is located in the relatively secularized university town of Saskatoon, Saskatchewan. When associate pastor Sam Chaise began to consider how to target Busters in Saskatoon, he realized that they would not be open to traditional church forms, especially in a town where churchgoers are a definite minority. Hence Chaise began The Alternative, an outreach event he describes as a "coffeehouse torqued up a bit." The Alternative, a monthly outreach, features lots of secular music that hints at spiritual reality, ample supplies of food and drink, a very short talk, and plenty of time for interaction. By and large, Busters do not want to be told what to believe. To accommodate this, Chaise provides a place where questions can be safely raised and answered with both asker and answerer on level ground.

The Alternative puts a strong emphasis on relational evangelism. The outreach is best understood, says Chaise, as a catalyst and help for previously existing relationships between Christians and their seeking friends. Because it is "pre-evangelism" rather than thorough teaching, The Alternative cannot stand alone without adequate follow-up.

Interestingly enough Sam Chaise does not use the terms "Baby Buster" or "Generation X" unless the person he is speaking with uses them first. "The generation does not want to be pigeonholed," he says, "and labels are a turn-off." Chaise plans to eventually implement a Saturday night worship service where new followers of Christ attracted by The Alternative can grow in their faith and their connectedness to the Christ-following community. But it is The Alternative that will draw many in the first place, a ministry that takes Buster culture seriously, particularly its desire for informality, its need for interactivity and relationship, and its music.

We will need to pay particular attention to music. It is difficult to overestimate the importance of music in the life of Busters; rock music has always been good at capturing and even nurturing the ethos of alienation and angst. Alternative rock music is probably the dominant Buster art form. Fortunately there are a number of fine alternative rock musicians and songwriters who come from a Christian perspective and speak powerfully to Busters. The late Mark Heard's bluesy acoustic folk-tinged rock powerfully addresses both despair and grace. The band The Choir sings about redemptive relationships in a world gone awry. Steve Taylor's relentless honesty and biting satire appeal to many Busters. Jars of Clay is a Christian band that is enjoying mainstream commercial success because of its direct, uncompromising, and authentic lyrics about faith, failure, and redemption. And the gifted Athens, Georgia-based mainstream band Vigilantes of Love communicates the message that "it is grace that allows us to view our brokenness and loneliness, and grace that allows us the possibility of hope in response, no matter how all-encompassing darkness might seem."[8] Those who want to minister to Busters will do well to know the alternative rock genre and to take advantage of this material in outreach contexts.

What is most important to understand is that effective ministers to Busters will not be frightened of cultural forms. Historically the Christian evangelical movement has tended to make one of two opposing mistakes when confronting the culture. The first is to *accommodate,* blindly following cultural dictates and dulling the unique sweetness and sometimes shocking tartness of the Christian message. The second is to *flee* from culture, choosing to reject all culture as bad. The result here has been churches mired in cultural forms from previous, more "holy" generations or, worse, a parallel Christian culture (inferior Christian art and music, not to mention Christian aerobics and fountain pens).

A better way is to *honor* and *use* the culture, learning it from the inside out and rejecting that which is intrinsically offensive to the Christian message while realizing that this offense should almost never occur, because God can take care of himself. In practical terms this may mean not being afraid of fast-moving visual imagery, raves, alternative rock, contemporary cinema, and even body art.

Change

We've gone to great lengths to show that Busters have inherited a postmodern world characterized by dizzying change and upheaval. While this change is disorienting and occasionally frightening, it can also be exhilarating. Busters tend to like change, sometimes for change's sake. In the world they live in, with the uncertainty of jobs and politics and relationships, they have little choice but to embrace change.

Churches that will reach Busters will not be afraid of change in philosophy, personnel, leadership style, and organizational personality. When Dieter Zander left New Song Church for Willow Creek, New Song replaced him with a team of pastors rather than going the traditional route of hiring a new senior pastor. This kind of "thinking outside the box" will be mandatory for effective Buster churches. We do not yet know if anyone is doing this effectively or not. Things are changing too fast to tell! We do know that the odds are against our success. Organizations and institutions tend to move inexorably toward a maintenance mode. Willow Creek Community Church's Boomer-oriented, seeker-targeted style of ministry, once seen as dangerously radical, is now commonly accepted and even feels a bit tame—to us at least. One day soon New Song Church will become the establishment as well. What then?

At Forest Hill Church the leadership of the Buster ministry says only half jokingly, "Change is a friend with whom you curl up on a cold winter's night." We must not only tolerate change, we must seek it out and embrace it. And yet we must not lose touch with our better traditions and historical rootedness. One senses that liturgy has a place in much Buster ministry. The Warehouse ministry in York, England, somehow brings together liturgy, incense, multimedia imagery, and techno music!

Rooted in a passionate commitment to the One who is "the same yesterday and today and forever" (Heb. 13:8) and to "the faith that was once for all entrusted to the saints" (Jude 3), those who minister effectively to Baby Busters will themselves not be afraid to challenge assumptions, disrupt organizational structures, shatter paradigms, and overhaul methodologies for ministry.

10

The Heroic Life

How the Mighty Have Fallen

After Saul and Jonathan, the great warriors and heroes of Israel, were killed in battle, David cried out three times, "How the mighty have fallen!" This could be our cry as well. Time and time again we see the heroes and icons of our culture, the mighty ones, fall into tragedy or disgrace.

Pete Rose, Mike Tyson, and O. J. Simpson immediately spring to mind when we think of fallen sports heroes. Scandals in Hollywood and Washington are literally too numerous to recount. Many of the religious superstars have fallen, brought down by sordid tales of sexual immorality and corruption. Even Superman, the ultimate hero of our culture, was killed off in the comics!

We have already spoken of Kurt Cobain as the embodiment of a hopeless generation. He also represents our sad aberration of heroism. While traveling to a university to speak about Baby Busters, we spent our time discussing the heroes of the generation. We both agreed that it would not be shocking if Cobain were dead within five years because of his long history of drug abuse and self-destructive behavior. The very next day, he was hospitalized for an overdose. Five weeks later he shot himself to death.

The tragic but unsurprising impact followed. At least two young men committed suicide in response to his death. Many Baby Busters reported feeling "totally destroyed" by the loss. National crisis hotlines reported an exponential increase in calls during the following weeks. High schools across the country had counselors on alert to talk with depressed students.

It was—in a quiet but profound way—a defining moment for the generation. Baby Busters now had their own tragic hero. The other heroes seemed invulnerable before they fell; Cobain's tragic end seemed almost inevitable.

Kurt Cobain was a hero for the generation because he somehow connected with the sense of being disconnected. He comforted those who shared his angst. In his death the generation has lionized him as a spokesman for the disaffected.

Uncovering the Passion for the Heroic

Kurt Cobain's status as a champion and spokesman for the generation says much about our view of heroes. It seems to suggest that the only heroes that we will embrace are those who represent pain, perhaps even frailty and weakness. The heroes who represent strength and virtue seem to disappoint us over and over. Cobain, while embodying honesty and frankness, stood as a symbol of one beaten down by life. In the end the story of his life has him crushed by his torments, not courageously struggling and persevering. It is hard to be disappointed by him. His senseless death seems to be the poignant but logical extension of his life.

During that same trip to the university, we picked up the daily student newspaper on campus and read a prominent second-page feature on how this generation is skeptical of heroes. We are afraid they will not live up to our expectations, the article claimed. It went on to say that we do not want to be heroes. We see the failings of our own heroes and, in reaction, do not want the responsibility or the burden of potentially disappointing others.

On the face of it, all of this sounds accurate. Busters are cautious, not wanting to trust others. As a generation we always expect to be disappointed. Consequently we avoid opportunities to disappoint others. Instead we take our risks in physically dangerous but interpersonally safe ways.

However, when you talk with Busters individually, when you really get to see our passion and desires, you understand that this facade is not true at all. Underneath all of the self-protective layers, we are deeply passionate people. We are people wanting to make a difference, wanting to touch others deeply. True, there is fear and uncertainty about how to do it, but there is a drive to better the world around us.

With this said, believing members of this generation need to hear this exhortation clearly: Live a heroic life; rescue the captives; make a unique impact.

Let's examine together each part of this exhortation to more fully develop what it means to live a heroic life.

Live a Heroic Life

Our concept of heroes has been largely formed from our youth. As with other generations, we grew up with fantasy heroes. For us it was Batman, Superman, and the rest of the superheroes. We associated special abilities or strength with heroism. A true hero, in our minds, was one who did good by means of this special ability. As kids we all longed for that special ability or often pretended we had it during our play.

However, few people in real life have extraordinary ability, so we redefined our concept of hero as we entered adolescence and adulthood, as other generations had before us. But unlike previous generations who redefined heroes as ones who stood up for some truth or ideal, we had a more difficult time. Our upbringing had robbed us of a strong sense of truth and shared virtue. Instead our hero became one who stood up to express a strong feeling, despite resistance or lack of acceptance from the mainstream.

In this sense Kurt Cobain fit the definition well. He expressed his feelings of alienation, rage, and despair, singing lines calculated to repulse the masses but sure to be embraced by those with whom the feelings hit home. To many he stood for some good things, but his appeal was built on the congruence of his emotions shared with those of his audience. It can be summed up in the quote, "He felt what I felt."

Clearly a fuller definition of what it means to be heroic is needed. A good definition is surprisingly simple: To be heroic means to be both courageous and noble. Both of these elements are necessary.

A courageous person is one who faces danger with confidence and resolution. The courageous person looks at danger with a certainty of mission and a determination not to back down until right prevails. Baby Busters have confused courage with foolish thrill seeking. True courage involves standing up to resistance and is usually found within the context of interpersonal relationships. Unlike our childhood views of courage, it rarely involves defusing a bomb or jumping over a canyon but often takes the decidedly messier form of getting involved in the dangerous business of relationships.

It is dangerous to risk being taken advantage of because of your mercy. It is dangerous to risk helping someone who may reject or attack you after you are no longer needed. It is dangerous to risk feeling the hurt of the deep wounds of others. Getting involved in relationships with others, particularly those who do not know God or those who are in pain or need, is messy and risky. It is not pretty nor is it always immediately gratifying, but it takes more courage than skydiving. As followers of Jesus we must commit ourselves to moving powerfully into the lives of others, risking rejection and scorn.

A hero is courageous, but a hero is also noble. A noble person is one who possesses high moral character. Something is moral if it is right or good and immoral if it is wrong or evil. Historically the divide between what was moral and immoral was determined by objective standards and rooted in the notion that there are certain absolute truths. With the challenge to objective truth, morality has taken a beating. Everyone is now free to determine what is right or wrong. Following one's own (ever changing, situational) moral code is commended, but there is no longer a sense that morality is built on certain foundational truths and beliefs.

As Christians we take comfort in the fact that God has given us reliable instruction in Scripture for living a noble life. He has also given us his Holy Spirit to guide and direct us. To be sure, there are still many times when our course of action is not clear or when we have to wrestle with tough moral dilemmas, but God has given us enough guidance and direction to know the limits and parameters. We are equipped with all that we need to live a noble life.

Living a noble life means living a life of personal integrity. Individually we are called to know and abide by the tenets of our faith. We are called to live in such a way that we stand out as distinct in any setting. The majority of people we know may live amoral or immoral lives, but we must individually commit ourselves to be different. Anything that is keeping us from living noble lives must be trashed. It must be taken out of our hearts or minds or patterns of behavior and thrown away. Do not tolerate it.

We are called to live heroic lives. We must, therefore, be both courageous and noble. We must be courageous by facing the danger and risk of moving boldly into the difficult business of relationships to meet needs and touch pain. We must be noble by living moral lives of personal integrity.

Rescue the Captives

Thinking again in terms of a story, we know that ultimately Jesus is the hero. Yet at the same time, we are called to be like him. For us this means acting heroically. The story is a cosmic rescue mission in which the captives have been lulled into complacency, often unaware of the horror of their plight or their imminent doom.

For those of us committed to living a heroic life, we not only move into the lives of others and touch felt needs, but we also move toward them with the conviction that they must ultimately be rescued.

Wartime stories abound of army medics who bandaged wounded soldiers amid enemy fire and mortar attacks.

It would not be enough to treat the wounds, however, and not provide a way for the injured man to be pulled into safety. The same is true for us. We move into the front lines and meet the needs and touch the pain, but we also keep focused on the ultimate need to pull the wounded into safety.

We know that despite the shift into postmodernism and the other societal changes that have occurred in the past thirty years, people still have a real and urgent need for a rescuer. They may not hear the enemy fire or sense the danger, but the need is still there. As believing members of this generation, we must have a passion for rescuing the captives. At school, on the job, during our workouts, we must feel the compelling need to introduce them to our Rescuer. If we first move toward them, demonstrating love and compassion in courageous, noble ways, we will feel even more compelled to rescue them. It will become the overflow of our hearts.

Make a Unique Impact

We are each called to display courage and integrity as we enter into the lives of others, addressing needs in the physical, emotional, and spiritual dimensions. The forms that this will take can be quite different. This is because each of us has different gifts and abilities that cause us to be used by God in many different ways.

Every believer is endowed by God with at least one supernatural enabling. It might be the ability to deeply encourage someone or help someone understand spiritual truth or demonstrate profound discernment. The Bible calls these enablings "spiritual gifts" (1 Cor. 12:1). In addition to spiritual gifts we have natural gifts and abilities, personality and temperament, and acquired skills. This unique array of gifts, abilities, and desires combines in a way that makes each of us as different as snowflakes or fingerprints. Some examples of how God works will make this point clear.

Marc is a twenty-year-old sociology major at a large university in the Northeast. He has been a Christian for seven years but has only begun to really grow since becoming involved in his fellowship group at school. He is realizing that he has a passionate desire to help poor, inner-city kids and has a great ability to communicate well with them. He wants to be a guidance counselor, but this summer he is going to work as an intern with an organization in Philadelphia that helps poor kids. He is going to play basketball with them during the day and lead them in Bible study during an afternoon break. He is also going to go into several of their homes to help do basic repairs, like patching holes and unclogging drains. Despite his desire to help the kids, going into these neighborhoods will be unsettling for him. He knows that the summer will be difficult in many ways.

Andrea is a twenty-five-year-old data processor for a healthcare firm. She is typically shy and introverted, but those who know her well say that she is a woman of tremendous spiritual depth. Recently she has been moved by stories of AIDS patients dying at hospices in her city and has felt God prompt her to volunteer. Most of the time when she goes, she does not know what to say. She just holds their hands or gets them something to drink. Lately she brings her portable computer and allows them to dictate messages to friends and family members. She senses in some of them a real desire to know God, so she shares with them the gospel and how God has changed her heart. Others are not interested in talking about spiritual things. She often leaves, however, feeling drained and despondent. She does not know whether to be angry or sad. Sometimes she is both.

Both stories reflect how God allows each of us individually to make a unique impact on the world around us. Marc and Andrea have different gifts, temperaments, abilities, and desires, yet God uses both of them in unique ways.

God has given you your own special assortment of talents and passions. Will you commit yourself to using what God has given you to make a unique impact on your world? As both of the stories also illustrate, making a unique impact is not without cost. Often the cost is emotional—fear, anger, sadness—and often it is in terms of time and resources. We must be so filled with our passion to make a unique impact that we are willing to do it at any cost.

Barriers to the Heroic Life

Living the heroic life is exhilarating and ultimately gratifying, but there are many barriers to it. Indeed the barriers to fully living out a heroic life are substantial. Many of these obstacles seem insurmountable at times. Thankfully, however, they are not. We are capable of effectively dealing with each of them.

Fear

The first barrier to the heroic life is fear. Fear can be a paralyzing emotion, rendering us immobile and ineffective. In striving to live out the heroic life, we will find ourselves compelled to move into the dangerous realm of intimate relationships. It is here that our fear often

Implications

grips us. We fear rejection. We fear conflict. We fear the unknown.

We are often afraid that our attempts to move toward others will be met with scorn or rebuff. Perhaps others, in their commitment to not appear needy, will push us away. Perhaps they will mock our faith. Perhaps we will be humiliated in front of peers or coworkers, or worse yet, talked about behind our backs, viewed as religious nuts. These are the things we all fear.

In relationships the fear of pain is also real and disturbing. Seeing others in pain is unsettling. Watching others reject our help can cause us anguish, as can the realization that we often do not have enough help to give. Being confronted by suffering and overwhelming need is painful, often causing us to despair. It challenges our hope. It is no wonder that most people do not choose to live heroic lives. It is too messy and painful—and often too frightening.

To overcome fear we must do three things. First, we have to understand our position in Christ. We have to become completely and deeply convinced that he loves us, that he will never let us go, and that he accepts us unconditionally. These understandings need to touch our hearts. Ironically this only happens when we put ourselves in risky and fearful situations. Then we find that God can be trusted to be good.

Second, we must allow our love and compassion for others to grow to the point of outweighing our anxiety. We must become so filled with mercy for others that their rejection, scorn, ridicule, or hostility is worth the price.

This brings to mind the story of a deeply disturbed young man. His parents had abandoned him when he was a young child, and his first foster family had abused him horribly. By the age of ten, he had already been in fifteen foster placements. Finally he was placed in a group home for children with emotional and behavioral problems. He was so filled with rage that he often had to be physically restrained to keep from hurting himself or others. Often during these restraints he would attempt to bite and scratch the staff member holding him. At least once he spit in the face of a woman who was gently restraining him. She returned to work again and again, never allowing his spitting, kicking, or cursing to keep her away. Each day she felt a knot in her stomach as she walked in the front door, never knowing whether she would be threatened and attacked. She said to another staff member, "If I can help him have a better life, then I don't mind getting spit on. I love this kid."

This true story serves as an effective metaphor for how strong love and compassion push us beyond our fear. We may not get spit on in the literal sense but quite possibly in the figurative. We may become the object of rage and open hostility, but we must become so filled with love for the hurting and needy that we are compelled to hold them anyway.

The third way to overcome fear requires us to return to the central premise of this book. We can have hope that God is actively working even now to bring a fragmented creation back together. To know this is to know that God is completely in control. How can we fear when we know that he is running the show? He is *God*.

Biblical Illiteracy

The second barrier to the heroic life is biblical illiteracy. Many may be surprised to see this regarded as a major obstacle to living a heroic life. Remember, however, that much of being heroic is being noble, and being noble means to possess moral character. We cannot have strong moral character without a consistent moral code. We must have strong moral instruction to know the boundaries of right and wrong conduct. In addition to giving us a glimpse of the character of God, Scripture provides that moral instruction for us.

In this age when many people consider themselves to be Christians, yet few can clearly articulate the major tenets of the faith, the need for biblical literacy among this generation is urgent. We must be a generation of believers who stand firmly grounded in and informed by Scripture. We must know what we believe and why we believe it. We must know how to study the Bible for ourselves and spend time soaking our thoughts in it.

In doing so we realize that God is not ours for the creating. Truth is not ours for the interpreting. Becoming biblically literate brings with it a fuller sense of the nature and character of God. It illuminates truth. It inspires us to act like Jesus—heroically.

Unconfessed Sin

The third barrier to the heroic life is unconfessed sin. When we do not repent of sin, we find it impossible to live in a way that is true to our own moral code. We often find ourselves plagued by guilt or feeling unworthy of acting in bold ways. Sin is like an irritant that rubs up against our conscience. It eventually must come out or it will rub us raw. Scripture calls this "searing the conscience." When this happens, we become numb to the effects and implications of our sin. We become callous to its destructive impact and, ultimately, are rendered impotent and powerless.

There have been many definitions of sin, but here we define it as anything that displeases and dishonors God. Failing to do something one should do or doing something one should not both qualify as sin. Our mission statement is to bring honor to God by the way we live our lives. In doing so we live out the heroic life. We cannot do this if we have not dealt effectively with our sin. Honor God by confessing and turning away from sin.

Selfishness

A final barrier to the heroic life is selfishness. It takes little argument to convince most people that we live in a narcissistic and self-centered culture. Our generation is not necessarily better or worse in this regard. As believers we constantly struggle with the messages that tell us to gratify ourselves and the call we have to live for others. We fight against the apathetic noninvolvement of many of our peers to become involved in ways that take us out of our comfort range. If we succumb to selfishness, either in the form of self-indulgence or apathy, we fail to live out the heroic life.

Each of these barriers is formidable, but each one can be overcome. The first step is becoming aware that these barriers exist and then developing a plan of attack. The plan may include seeking outside accountability, developing a structured regimen of daily Bible study, or pushing ourselves to do something that is in our heart but outside of our comfort zone. Each of us is able to take some action to overcome the barriers that keep us from fully living a heroic life.

Examine your own heart. What is keeping you from living life with reckless hope and heroic abandon? Is it your fear? Is it your lack of good moral instruction and guidance? Is it your unconfessed sin? Is it your selfishness? What is holding you back? Find it and drive it out of your life.

Implications

Follow the Hero

Busters have grown up without heroes and without an understanding of the heroic. Jenny Lyn Bader writes, "My generation helped kill off heroism as teenagers, with our language. We used heroic words that once described brave deeds—excellent, amazing, awesome—to describe a good slice of pizza or a sunny day. In our everyday speech, bad meant good. Hot meant cool. In the sarcastic slang of street gangs in Los Angeles, hero currently means traitor."[1] Our generation has no sense of what it means to be heroic. The heroes for the Buster generation were absent, defective, or are now gone.

In a sense clearing the field of heroes may be a good development. Jesus can now stand alone. He was courageous; he stood up to the Pharisees and he went willingly to his death to save others. He was noble; he taught us what it means to live a life that is pleasing to God. He lived a life of complete integrity. Jesus can be held out as the hero for the generation. He is also our model to follow as we strive to live the heroic life.

Jesus, however, is more than just a good role model. He is fully God. Many have tried to reduce Jesus to being just a good example for how to live, stripping him of his divinity. He is our role model, our example, our hero, but he is also our Lord. We must live in full obedience to him.

Heroes Create Heroes

When we act heroically, it often inspires others to do the same. We raise the standard as well as the level of passion. As believing members of our generation, we are called to stir others to heroic lives.

Here is a tremendous story: In Victor Hugo's *Les Misérables,* the hero, Jean Valjean, released after being imprisoned for many years, steals a basket of silver belonging to a bishop who had shown him only kindness and hospitality. The police almost immediately arrest Valjean and bring him back to the bishop. How does the bishop respond after being symbolically spit in the face by this ungrateful man? He tells the police to let him go, tells Valjean the basket of silver is now his to keep, and hands him two silver candlesticks as well. As the police loosen their grip on him and walk away, the priest says, "Jean Valjean, my brother: you belong no longer to evil, but to good. It is your soul that I am buying for you. I withdraw it from dark thoughts and from the spirit of perdition and I give it to God."[2] Jean Valjean goes on to become a true hero, both courageous and noble. It took the willingness of a believer, though, to kindle his spirit. He lived a heroic life because someone acted heroically toward him. As believers we are called to move beyond a marginalized existence and live with nobility and courage.

Here again is your charge: Live a heroic life; rescue the captives; make a unique impact. May God be honored.

The Final Charge

We started out covering familiar territory. We told you who we are as a generation and how we got to be that way. We told you how Christians managed to miss the generation and how the church is losing its footing as the dominant influence in our culture.

We then turned to Scripture and saw how God is in the business of putting a fractured world back together. He is firmly in control, and because of that we have Hope. We discussed how the concept of story and storytelling is the most important medium for reaching our generation. Then we examined important core themes for reaching Baby Busters—creation, covenant, and community— and considered the implications of these "operating values." We gave examples of how some innovative churches and other ministries are already reaching Baby Busters. Finally we demonstrated the need to exhort the members of our generation to live heroically.

Our challenge has been to provide you with information about the Baby Buster generation while exhorting you to put it into practice. We want you to go beyond understanding and move to action.

If you are not a Buster, we want you to have developed a heart for Busters. We want you to not only understand them but move toward them with the hope of Jesus. We want you to challenge them and call them to live for something greater than themselves.

If you are a Buster, we want you to be excited about your own generation and committed to living your own heroic life. The potential and challenge before you is enormous. Our generation is both frustrating and thrilling.

The Workers Are Few

Regardless of your generational affiliation, we leave you with one last charge. It is a charge that Jesus gave to his disciples before he sent them out. It is a charge to pray fervently that God would send workers out to reach those who do not know him.

When Jesus was actively moving through the culture of his day, teaching about the kingdom of God, he would come upon the masses of people in each town. In Matthew 9:36–38, Scripture says this:

> When he saw the crowds, he had compassion on them, because they were harassed and helpless, like sheep without a shepherd. Then he said to his disciples, "The harvest is plentiful but the workers are few. Ask the Lord of the harvest, therefore, to send out workers into his harvest field."

The modern church has often lacked compassion for the crowds, seeing them as harassing, not harassed; harmful, not helpless. The truth is that this generation, like the generation in Jesus' day, is like a flock of scared sheep without a shepherd.

Notice Jesus' instructions to his followers. He says, in essence, "There is a huge harvest of souls in front of you, but there are not enough workers out there among them. Pray that God will send out the workers." His admonition to them was first and foremost to pray.

This is our final charge: Pray! Pray that God would send out workers to work for a harvest among this generation. Pray that Christians would cease attempting to seize political power but, rather, would take the bigger risk of moving into personal relationships with those who do not know God. Pray that God would raise up young men and women from within the generation who want to live heroically.

The Harvest Fields

In the passage from Matthew 9, the harvest field is understood to be the world in general. There are, however, specific, smaller harvest fields. As we pray for God to raise up workers, we also pray that they would move into specific harvest fields. Here are our offerings for three harvest fields that are on our hearts. There may be others toward which you sense God's leading.

Race Relations

It has become more than a sad truism that the most segregated hour of the week is on Sunday mornings. It reflects the heart of the church in our culture. We must be completely frank about this point: Racism in any form is sin and is abhorrent to God.

Some churches allow members to make flagrantly racist comments and jokes without confronting or disciplining them. Those types of racist attitudes are easy to identify. However, most of the racism takes more subtle forms. Our failure to reach out to others of different races is something about which we also must repent.

The races continue to regard each other with fear and hatred, often blaming and accusing each other. The church has done seemingly little to stop this. While there are many hopeful signs of local churches becoming racially balanced and involved, this is not the overall trend.

It is likely that race relations will continue to worsen over the next few years. We are becoming increasingly polarized and divided from each other as fear and hatred grow. There seems little room for dialogue or chance for reconciliation. The church cannot afford to avoid this issue any longer. We must confront it directly. Busters who know the reconciling love of Jesus must move out into this harvest field and speak words of hope. Pray that God would raise up leaders of all races who are committed to reconciliation. Pray that there would be a new generation of believers who hurdle the barriers of fear and hatred and risk involvement with people of other races.

Family Service

People from every generation agree that the traditional family is in desperate trouble. Since 1961, the year that the first Busters were born, the divorce rate has doubled, the number of children raised in single-parent homes has tripled, and the number of illegitimate births has increased by 400 percent. The reports of child abuse and neglect have also skyrocketed during this period.

The effects of family disintegration are profound. There seems to be an obvious, logical connection between family disintegration and the increasing rates of violent crime and declining moral standards. Karl Zinmeister of the American Enterprise Institute says, "There is a mountain of scientific evidence showing that when families disintegrate, children often end up with intellectual, physical and emotional scars that persist for life. . . . We talk about the drug crisis, the education crisis, and the problem of teen pregnancy and juvenile crime. But all these ills trace back to one source: broken families."[1]

Busters, while recognizing the breakdown of the traditional family, have come to accept many definitions of family as viable. Barna reports that only 19 percent of Busters consider a family to be a group of individuals to whom one is closely related, by either marriage or blood lines. The remaining 81 percent have accepted all kinds of alternatives, with the largest group (28 percent) defining a family as "people with whom you have close relationships or deep personal/emotional bonds."[2] These attitudes, no doubt born out of their own early experiences with broken families, are nonetheless ultimately harmful. These vague views of the concept of family serve to further undermine and weaken families.

Believers of our generation must actively work to counteract the destructive ideas about families that our peers hold. At the same time we must do the work of helping families in need. Pray that God would raise up workers to move into this harvest field. Pray that he would send many members of our generation to assist families who are at risk of falling apart. Pray that he would send many who have both perseverance and vision to strengthen families, particularly those in poverty and those in inner cities.

Education

Next to families schools are the most important socializing institutions in our culture. The beliefs and values of individuals are shaped here, particularly in higher education. Many of those values make their way into public policy a generation or two later. Educators can have a profound influence on the overall development of their students.

Recent trends in education, at both the public school and university levels, have angered many Christians. The response so far has been to publicly attack public education, express outrage at school board meetings, and take other adversarial action. Just as individual change happens from the inside out, change in systems and institutions happens the same way. The educational system will not change by external forces pressuring it. It will only change if there are forces at work on the inside that help to shape it. This is not to suggest that we need covert infiltration. We simply need more believers to work within education, not only to influence individual students but to create change in the values and ideas held by the whole system of academia.

Christian education that is separate from either public or other secular education serves a valuable function in our culture. However, we must come to terms with the fact that there are legions of students for whom Christian education will never be an option. We cannot be content with educating our kids in Christian schools and colleges and not moving into the public high schools and state universities to sway those systems. We should not abdicate our potential for ministry there or confuse external pressure with internal influence. We must become an active part of the academic system.

The goal should never be to make public education into Christian education but rather to move into a harvest field where minds are open and willing to consider diverse ideas. Pray that God would raise up members of this generation who feel compelled to move into the harvest field of secular education.

The True Power

Notice that our focus here is on prayer, not on activism. In the 80s and again in recent years, many evangelical Christians, sensing negative trends in the culture, have attempted to band together and flex their collective political muscle. Proponents of this type of political involvement offer seemingly compelling arguments: The church was not politically passive in the face of Nazism in Germany or slavery in the United States, and so on.

Our argument is not against any of the position statements offered by evangelical activists. Instead we challenge the members of our generation not to put their hope in the political process. Doing so reflects a small view of God. It takes greater courage to commit to a lifestyle of prayer, yet that is where the true power is found.

To paraphrase 2 Chronicles 7:14, this generation of young believers will see God respond when they humble themselves, pray, and commit to living noble and courageous lives. When we do this, God himself will forgive sins and bring healing to this land.

God is powerful and in control. Our greatest work is not in activism but in prayer. Through prayer God will raise up individuals who are carried along by his Spirit to move out into the harvest fields. When we become a generation fervently committed to prayer, we will see God work in awesome ways.

We All Need God

As we close we trust that you will pray and go—go into whatever harvest field God has put on your heart. We believe that the harvest is plentiful! If you need further convincing, read another powerful quote from Douglas Coupland as he concludes his almost tragic book, *Life after God:*

> Now—here is my secret: I tell it to you with an openness of heart that I doubt I shall ever achieve again, so I pray that you are in a quiet room as you hear these words. My secret is that I need God—that I am sick and can no longer make it alone. I need God to help me give, because I am no longer capable of giving; to help me be kind, as I no longer seem capable of kindness; to help me love, as I seem beyond being able to love.[3]

These are strong words from the man who has literally defined the generation. We believe that our generation is teeming with individuals who know they need God. They know they are sick and can no longer make it on their own. These are individuals who are ripe, ready to meet the Lord of the harvest if the workers come to show the way. This is a generation ready for hope.

Notes

Chapter 1: *Meet the Generation*

1. Alexander Star, "The Twentysomething Myth," *The New Republic* (January 4–11, 1993): 22–25.

2. Douglas Rushkoff, *The GenX Reader* (New York: Ballantine, 1994), 3.

3. Susan Mitchell, "How to Talk to Young Adults," *American Demographics* (April 1993): 51.

4. Douglas Coupland, *Generation X: Tales for an Accelerated Culture* (New York: St. Martin's Press, 1991), 11.

5. George Barna, *The Invisible Generation: Baby Busters* (Chicago: Northfield Publishing, 1992), 35.

6. Charlene Marmer Solomon, "Managing the Baby Busters," *Personnel Journal* (March 1992): 54.

7. Neil Howe and Bill Strauss, *13th Gen: Abort, Retry, Ignore, Fail?* (New York: Vintage Books), 9.

8. Barna, *The Invisible Generation*, 35.

9. Howe and Strauss, *13th Gen*, 11.

10. Mitchell, "How to Talk to Young Adults," 51.

Chapter 2: *Understand the Generation*

1. Joseph Spear, *Poor, Poor Generation X*, Newspaper Enterprise Assoc., 1994.

2. Rushkoff, *The GenX Reader*, 7.

Chapter 4: *Bringing It All Together*

1. We recommend a careful concordance study of phrases such as "last days."

2. The standard introduction to Eastern Orthodoxy is Timothy Ware's *The Orthodox Church* (London: Penguin, 1981).

3. Lawrence J. Crabb, *Finding God* (Grand Rapids: Zondervan, 1993), 33.

Chapter 5: *Living between the Already and the Not Yet*

1. Anthony Hoekema, *The Bible and the Future* (Grand Rapids: Eerdmans, 1979), 45.

2. See, for example: George Beasley-Murray, *Jesus and the Kingdom of God* (Grand Rapids: Eerdmans, 1986).

3. The D-Day illustration is drawn from the classroom lectures of Dr. G. K. Beale, Gordon-Conwell Theological Seminary, 1991.

4. Hoekema, *The Bible and the Future,* 73.

Chapter 6: *Hope for the Hopeless*

1. John Leland, "Do You Hear What I Hear?" *Newsweek* (January 27, 1992): 39–45.

2. *Rolling Stone* (June 2, 1994) is a helpful and poignant retrospective of Cobain's life and brief career.

3. Correspondence, Love Letters, and Advice, *Rolling Stone* (June 2, 1994): 11.

4. Letters, *Details* (June 1994).

5. Douglas Coupland, *Life after God* (New York: Pocket Books, 1994).

6. Ibid., 183–84.

7. Illustration drawn from a talk given by Paul Borthwick at regional ACMC conference at Columbia, South Carolina, in June 1993.

Chapter 7: *Telling the Old New Story*

1. Coupland, *Generation X,* 8.

2. Robert Jenson, "How the World Lost Its Story," *First Things* 36 (1993): 19–24.

3. Crabb, *Finding God,* 200.

4. Eugene Peterson, *The Message: New Testament* (Colorado Springs: Nav-Press, 1994).

5. Leighton Ford, *The Power of Story* (Colorado Springs: NavPress, 1994), 10. See also Kevin Ford, *Jesus for a New Generation* (Downers Grove, Ill.: InterVarsity Press, 1995), for a fine discussion of a "narrative apologetic."

6. Crabb, *Finding God,* 191.

Chapter 8: *Operating Values for the Generation*

1. William B. Badke, *Project Earth: Preserving the World God Created* (Portland: Multnomah, 1991).

Chapter 9: *Putting It in Place*

1. William Mahedy and Janet Bernardi, *A Generation Alone* (Downers Grove, Ill.: InterVarsity, 1994), 84.

2. Jan Johnson, "Getting the Gospel to the Baby Busters," *Moody* (May 1995): 48–53.

3. Mahedy and Bernardi, *A Generation Alone,* 74.

4. Ibid., 70.

5. Zander's audio tape *Reaching Baby Busters* is available from Willow Creek Church's Seeds Tape Ministry as item WCA851: (708) 765-0070.

6. George G. Hunter III, *How to Reach Secular People* (Nashville: Abingdon Press, 1992), 74.

7. Johnson, "Getting the Gospel to the Baby Busters," 49.

8. From the liner notes to the band Vigilantes of Love's 1995 album *Blister Soul,* written by Thom Jurek.

Chapter 10: *The Heroic Life*

1. Jenny Lyn Bader, "Larger Than Life," in *Next: Young American Writers on the New Generation,* ed. Eric Liu (New York: W. W. Norton, 1994), 11–12.

2. Victor Hugo, *Les Misérables,* trans. Charles E. Wilbour (New York: Fawcett, 1961), 39.

Chapter 11: *The Final Charge*

1. Karl Zinmeister, quoted in *The Index of Leading Cultural Indicators,* ed. William Bennett (New York: Simon & Schuster, 1994), 45.

2. Barna, *The Invisible Generation,* 114.

3. Coupland, *Life after God,* 359.

About the Authors

Todd Hahn has an M.Div. from Gordon-Conwell Theological Seminary. He is the associate pastor for outreach at Forest Hill Church in Charlotte, North Carolina. He is author of the study guide for the paperback edition of *Transforming Leadership* by Leighton Ford.

David Verhaagen has a Ph.D. in psychology from the University of North Carolina-Chapel Hill. He is a child psychologist and the clinical director for a mental health agency that serves children and families. He is author of several professional journal articles.